POTTERY FOR BEGINNERS

POTTERY FOR BEGINNERS

Harold Powell

BLANDFORD PRESS

Poole   Dorset

First published in 1978
by Blandford Press Ltd,
Link House, West Street,
Poole, Dorset,
BH15 1LL
Copyright © Blandford Press 1978

To Dorothy, a potter's wife

British Library Cataloguing in Publication Data
Powell, Harold
    Pottery for beginners.
    1. Pottery craft
    I. Title
    738.1   TT920

ISBN 0-7137-0910-3

Printed in Great Britain by
Butler & Tanner Ltd, Frome and London

Contents

Introduction

I have just been reading a newspaper report about a pottery exhibition which took place over twenty years ago. The work was the combined efforts of two weekly classes, and the reporter commented upon the two hundred and fifty models on view. I have some photographs of that exhibition and I am impressed by the variety and colour of those exhibits. Some school, college and evening institute teachers might be surprised at the volume of work which the students produced, all from one medium-sized kiln which was also used for day students. Clays used were white body, buff, Staffordshire red, grogged clays and pink and blue stained clays. You may note the absence of stoneware clay. Had stoneware been fired the volume of work would have been gradually reduced for the life of the kiln elements would have been considerably shortened.

One question will spring to the minds of readers immediately; what of the quality of the work? One sets one's own standards, and the value of the work was probably in the variety of processes attempted without copying the ideas of established potters or industrialists.

This brings me to an important point which I should like to make to my readers.

On many of my visits to assist educational potters I have been dismayed at the lack of variety in the work offered. In senior establishments stoneware pottery has been predominant. Where it was good it was very very good. But so often colour and glaze decoration had been sacrificed for the fashion of high temperature firing.

I believe the pottery syllabus should cover a wide area of pottery activity. Coil, slab, slip cast, wheel, figure modelling, abstract modelling; all these areas plus all the decorative processes which are available to the progressive potter.

I would suggest too that teachers demonstrate skills and methods as often as possible, and aim to make as many lessons as possible successful when work will be fired and glazed. Success does not come often to a group in a corner given a lump of clay and told to make something.

This is of paramount importance to the teachers of evening classes. How many times have numbers dwindled between September and December because students have become discouraged.

So, my sojourn into the past reminds me that it is the enthusiasm of teachers which gives initial progress and as students struggle to master techniques strange to them they are encouraged by the slightest success.

Perhaps today, with advanced technology at our disposal, and a wealth of pottery materials available, our enthusiasm for experiment may have been 'dented' a little.

My book may help to remind you of simple techniques and supply hints and ideas and some technical advice which may assist you as beginners.

The pottery craft has grown at a very fast rate over these twenty years to which I referred earlier, and the technical ability of some of our Studio potters, and our Educational potters is excellent.

If you are a beginner or a more experienced potter I trust my book may be of some help and I wish you successful and 'Happy Potting'.

Clays

Readers of this book whose pottery experience in schools goes back to the 1950s may remember the difficulties in obtaining good workable clay. Clay was delivered with other art materials, not arriving until months after the order had been given, wrapped in brown paper and as solid as a rock. Special permission was granted by the education authorities in some areas for industrial merchants to be approached for supplies which would be ready to use. It was no uncommon sight to receive a wooden barrel containing up to 200 kg (4 cwt) of clay, and no uncommon sight to see small boys hanging head-first inside the barrel scraping the remnants of clay from the bottom.

All that has changed, and we can be grateful for the service we have received from the clay-merchants. Once these suppliers learned of the needs of schools and colleges in the way of materials and tools they reacted splendidly to meet these needs. Whilst it was good fun and, it must be supposed, educational to use soft unfired bricks from the brickyard and clay dug from the school field or brought to school from street excavations, it certainly added to the difficulties of teachers when the clay had to be cleaned and prepared. Also the amounts which were required to serve large classes were not available from these sources.

Now there are adequate supplies of prepared clays and many variations in earthenware, stoneware, china and porcelain. There are grogged clays, ovenware clays and clays in powder form for the craft of slip decoration. The purpose of this chapter is to help select these clays for school and hobby potting.

Staffordshire Red Clay

The marl or terracotta clays, now usually referred to as Staffordshire Red, are ideal clays for throwing, coiling and general modelling. Experienced potters often use the term 'kind clays' because of the modelling qualities of the clay. Mined in Etruria in the 'Potteries' district from a quarry which has supplied industry for 150 years, it was used to make those attractive tea-pots that graced every British working class home.

One supplier prepares the clay in two ways. The first is a pure Staffordshire Red clay which when made into a slip is sieved, filtered, pugged and ready for use. The clay fires to a pleasant terracotta pink at 960°C. and matures between 1020°C. and 1100°C. At a higher temperature the biscuit would be quite dark, and possibly difficult to make the glaze adhere, so that a more workable temperature for glost firing is no higher than 1060°C. at the biscuit stage. If thinly potted the clay could warp at the higher temperature range.

The second preparation of Staffordshire Red clay matures at a temperature of 1160°C. because of the addition of ball clay which makes the clay more stable. Again a lower temperature, certainly below 1100°C., is preferable for successful glaze firing.

Staffordshire Red clay may be decorated with slips or glazes. A coil pot with thumbed or modelling-stick decoration sealing the coils to each other is most attractively decorated by dipping into tin glaze, and, whilst the glaze is in powder form on the pot, rubbing the prominent markings gently to remove some of the glaze. When fired the tin glaze fills the depressions and coil joinings, and where the glaze has been rubbed the shiny brown of the clay breaks through.

Buff clay

The large slab pots illustrated in this book were made from buff grogged clay, known in one catalogue as buff school clay. The clay is grogged with 10 per cent. of sand, which helps it to dry and fire without warping. This clay is ideal for modelling since fairly large, thick pieces may be built or modelled without fear of explosion in the kiln, always of course depending upon the preparation of the clay either by pugging or wedging. (Even the smallest piece of clay which encloses an air bubble will explode as it is heated in the kiln.) Buff grogged clay has other advantages: it is excellent for throwing and has a wide temperature range since the base is prepared from fire-clay. This is a useful asset for schools for it may be fired at earthenware or stoneware temperatures 1100°C.–1280°C.

White earthenware body

A white earthenware body is so named because of the non-plastic ingredients it contains. It is now a standard body which was originally developed by the famous eighteenth century potters, including the legendary Josiah Wedgwood. Every student of pottery history will have studied the development of this first white English clay, when for a time the English potters superseded the production of domestic pottery in Europe. It made possible new forms of decoration such as underglaze and on-glaze transfers, and on-glaze painted decoration. Today it provides school and hobby potters with a clay which is ideal for the craft of mosaics, agate ware and tile making. In powder form it is deflocculated into a casting slip for pouring into plaster moulds and, when prepared as a thick slip and stained with pottery colourants, enables potters to practise a technique known as slip trailing.

White earthenware body matures between 1100°C. and 1150°C., but can be fired and glazed successfully at 1060°C.–1070°C. The composition is as follows:—Ball clay 25 per cent., China clay 25 per cent., Flint 35 per cent. and China stone 15 per cent. These minerals are mixed with water and put into an 'arc', a large tank in which a paddle revolves, rather like a washing machine. It is then sieved, passed over magnets to remove iron deposits, and finally filtered and pugged.

This composition has excellent throwing properties, and is good for modelling if kept constantly damp. It is possible, particularly with slip-cast pottery to 'once fire' this clay; this means drying, glazing and firing in one operation.

Stoneware clays

So far, the clays mentioned have been earthenware clays and the clays used in the main by school potters. But of course high firing stoneware clay is very popular with Studio potters and in some senior schools. There is a strange fascination about stoneware firing, and some potters hold the theory that because of the high firing required to mature stoneware clays the clay is in some way reverting to its original rock form; that is before its igneous and decomposed state. Whether this is valid or not the process of firing and glazing demands much skill and knowledge of both glaze and clay.

Unfortunately this fascination can lead to badly glazed and decorated stoneware. Unless it is in the hands of experienced potters the results by some school and evening institute pottery classes can be intensely disappointing.

Perhaps beginners in this field should rely upon the prepared stoneware glazes sold by the pottery suppliers: well-known potters such as David Leach, Derek Emms and Harry Stringer all allow their glazes to be made available through one of these suppliers. When a muffle kiln is available then the method known as reduction is probably the most rewarding of stoneware decoration. The atmosphere of the kiln is reduced of its oxygen content by burning gas towards the end of the firing cycle. This has the effect of changing the normal colouring of oxides. It requires much practice and knowledge of oxides to achieve success, but the results can be very dramatic and very rewarding.

However, with Harry Stringer's Taggs Yard glaze and slip techniques the effects of reducing can be copied in an oxidizing kiln atmosphere. Briefly, the technique is to fire the vessel to a low biscuit firing as with all stoneware clays and dip it into a prepared black slip. This can also be done at the leather-hard stage and is known as a reactive slip. An hour after dipping, the pot may be glazed with Mr. Stringer's transparent or Tenmoko/Chun glazes, and fired between 1250°C. and 1280°C. The results when correctly applied are very exciting.

There is also an earthenware clay which would be suitable for many Primary schools where there is a small kiln with a low temperature range. This is a low firing clay whose maturing temperature is between 960°C. and 1060°C. Even at the lower temperature of 960°C. and using the specially prepared low firing glaze the clay can be compared favourably with the higher temperature earthenware clays. If used in a large kiln the temperature should not be taken above 1060°C. The cobalt in the clay gives it a white appearance at low temperature, but if fired too high changes the whiteness to grey.

There are other clays too when the beginner gains experience, and decides to leave the comparative safe haven of limited pottery techniques. But the best advice any potter might give to the beginner is to proceed cautiously and seek advice from the craft pottery suppliers who give technical service and provide seminars for those wishing to improve their knowledge. It is tempting when reading about the apparently simple technique of Raku firing, for instance, to attempt it in an electric kiln, but this should be attempted only by absolute experts. Pots may be made from a buff clay, fired in the ordinary way and decorated with oxides and a prepared frit. They are then placed in a muffle kiln whilst the temperature is around 800°C. The pots are removed when they are red-hot and plunged into sawdust. This action produces a reducing atmosphere around the oxides and often dramatic colour patterns. Having suggested some clays which will serve you well, now is the time to write about the care of clay.

Care of clay

As soon as clay is removed from its plastic covering, or from the clay-bin the process of hardening begins. Warm hands and a warm room begin to take the moisture from the clay. This of course is within your experience even as beginners, and you take steps to make your model whilst the clay is still soft.

If you wish to delay the finish of your model you must protect it from warm dry air, either by placing it in a damp cupboard, or enclosing it in a plastic bag. If neither of these is at hand the clay model may be covered with a damp cloth, but of course the cloth must be re-dampened occasionally if it begins to dry.

A damp cupboard is either an airtight wooden cupboard lined with zinc, or a metal cabinet; and the pottery is placed on plaster slabs which have been soaked in water.

Clay which has been left over from modelling and is becoming hard will require some treatment to return it to its former plastic state. Here is how you might achieve this:

1 Unused clay on the bench or table could be kept in a wet paper towel or cloth during the lesson.

2 For infant or junior classes where a bag of clay is stored in a bin in the classroom, you could ask the children to roll the clay into balls and place each ball in a wet paper towel or cloth. If stored in paper towels these should be renewed frequently or the paper will disintegrate and become part of the clay.

3 If a large quantity of clay is used and stored in a senior school or college the clay (other than clay stored in plastic bags) is best kept in a metal lidded bin. Metal refuse bins are suitable. The clay should be 'spaded' every day. In effect this means returning used clay to the bin, chopping it finely with a spade and sprinkling with water. Do not use too much water or the clay will become sticky and difficult to reconstitute. If this should happen then it must be pugged with the addition of some harder clay or pressed and wedged on plaster bats until the excess water is removed—a very messy business.

Finally, do please check the delivery of clay. When clay is sent out from the merchant it is effectively sealed inside a thick plastic bag and will stay soft for months. But should the bag be damaged and clay exposed to the air it will rapidly become solid.

Coil Pottery

You are about to make your first clay model for firing, and it is important that you should achieve some measure of success. It is important also that you should learn some pottery skills, and so a choice must be made as to which type of model would be most suitable to meet these requirements.

One traditional method of making simple pots is to build up coils of clay. The rings or coils of clay are rolled by hand, and placed one on top of another until a reasonable height has been reached. Six or seven coils of 10 mm ($\frac{3}{8}$ in) thickness will do for your first attempt. Later you will learn to control the clay coils and make varied shapes and sizes.

1 Huge coil pot made in Portugal.

2 *Starting off the coil.*

3 *Rolling with fingers spread.*

4 *Completed coil.*

5 *Ready for fixing.*

Practise rolling even coils—this is an important skill to learn if your pots are to fire successfully. Almost all beginners tend to roll 'square coils'. To counter this tendency the clay should be rolled upon a firm level surface and the palms of the hands should press and roll with even pressure throughout the movement. Try a standing position and, leaning over the table slightly, tuck your elbows close into your body and roll with long even strokes. If the clay flattens on two sides, pat it back into shape and continue rolling.

Final shaping of the coils should be made by the tips of the fingers, starting in the centre and stroking gently towards the ends of the coil. The coils must be rolled fairly quickly, for all clays will crack if rolled in a heated room with warm hands.

Materials and tools

Staffordshire Red clay; liquid clay (slip clay); paint brush; rolling pin and rolling guides; cutting tool or template; modelling board or bench whirler; sugar paper.

Single coil pot

Choose 10 mm ($\frac{3}{8}$ in) rolling guides and form a base of 10 mm ($\frac{3}{8}$ in) thick. Cut it using any round shape as a guide. If a wheel is available then the disc is easily cut from a slab of clay placed in the centre of the wheel; hold a needle—preferably fixed in a cork handle—over the slab, bring it gently down to the surface of the clay, and finally press down whilst the wheel head is turning. The disc will be cut quickly and cleanly. There are now, of course, special tile cutters available from suppliers which cut and extrude the discs very efficiently.

Now that the base is ready you may start to roll your first coil, but first ensure that tools and slip clay are to hand for fixing and sealing. Cross-hatch the edges of the disc with the pointed end of a modelling tool, and paint over with clay slip. Roll the first coil slightly oversize and cut one end at an angle. Place it in position on the base, level with the edge of the base, the uncut end overlapping the angled end. Checking the position of the angled end, now cut the overlapping coil to match (see Fig. 6). Paint each end with slip and press and join together.

6 Cutting at 45° angle.   *7 Sealing between coil
and base.*

Now place a thinner coil between base and coil and model
smoothly to form a sealed base. Before adding a second coil flatten
the first one by gently tapping with a modelling board and paint
the slightly flattened surface with clay slip. Follow the same procedure as with the first coil and build the pot up with six or seven
coils keeping the shape as straight as possible.

If the coils are even and fixed firmly with slip, then the pot should
dry and fire without cracking. But, as all potters know, any weak-
ness in the wall of a pot may lead to excess shrinking of the drying
clay and may result in cracking when the kiln reaches a high temperature. Therefore it is sometimes necessary to reinforce the coils
by inserting between each a thinner coil and modelling into position.
This is done inside the pot to form a smooth even finish.

There are alternative methods of sealing which you might try. The
first is achieved by pouring thick slip into the pot, and then decant-
ing. This could form part of your decoration if a contrasting coloured
slip were used. Another decorative method of sealing the outside of
the coils can be achieved by incising, i.e. pinching two coils together
with a modelling tool (see Fig. 12).

8 *Smoothing sealing coil.*

9 *Slip sealing ready for next coil.*

10 *Completed pot being sealed with liquid clay.*

11 *Slip decoration.*

When the skills of rolling and fixing coils are mastered, and several straight pots made and decorated, you will wish to add shape to your models. To widen a pot for a vase or bowl shape, make the second and subsequent coils slightly larger. When the extent of the bulge is reached make the coils slightly smaller until the desired shape and height is reached. Do not, of course, attempt too rapid a widening or narrowing of the pot so that the coils lean perilously outward or inward of the coil beneath. Whenever widening or narrowing is attempted it is necessary to seal each coil firmly before adding other coils.

Step by Step
Summary of Method

1 **Using thoroughly wedged clay roll and cut base. Roll on sugar paper between rolling guides.**

2 **Cut base with tool or around a template, or on the throwing wheel. Cross-hatch and paint edges with slip.**

3 **Roll coils oversize and cut one at an angle.**

4 **Place coil in position, slightly overlapping, cut, paint with slip and join.**

5 **Insert sealing coil between first coil and base.**

6 **Flatten first coil slightly, paint with slip and add further coils sealing with thinner coils as the pot rises.**

7 **When building the pot the coil joins must be staggered, i.e. they must not be one above the other or the pot will weaken down one side.**

Decoration

Tin glaze decoration

If the pots are made from Staffordshire Red clay tin glaze decoration is probably the most attractive. When the pot is fired to biscuit at around 1040°C. it may be dipped in tin glaze. The prominent markings left by the modelling tool should be rubbed lightly with the fingers to remove some of the glaze. When glost fired (1060°C.) brown markings will contrast against the tin white.

Using this method again with incised marked pots dipped in tin

12 Joining the coils with incise decoration.

13 Tin glazed ready for oxide decoration.

14 First dip of trailed pot.

15 Second dip.

glaze, paint each depression made by the sealing mark with a stain
or oxide on top of the raw tin glaze.

Slip decoration

When the coiling is finished and the pot is in leather-hard condition,
it may be decorated with coloured slips. First pour slip into the pot
and decant. Using a bottle or slip trailer filled with coloured slips,
trail lines of slip down the side of the pot. After biscuit firing dip
the pot is transparent glaze and fire again. Observe firing temperatures as in previous glaze decoration.

Preparation of materials

White and stained clays

Half a litre (1 pt) of water added to half a kilo (1 lb) of white clay
powder will produce a thin slip. For slip trailing, however, a much
thicker slip is necessary. So, mix and sieve through a 40s, or 60s sieve,
and allow the mixture to stand for several hours. You will notice
that much of the water in the solution has risen to the top of the
container. Decant this and check the consistency. Now mix and sieve
the stain or oxide to be used through a 120s sieve. When both colour
and liquid clay are re-sieved the mixture should be sufficiently thick
to require only slight pressure from the bottle or slip trailer to
extrude.

All your colours should be mixed with white clay for best results.
The clay may be bought in powder form or, if white plastic clay is
stocked, small pieces of the clay may be dried on top of the kiln when
firing and then crushed into powder ready for mixing with water.
When black slip is required for decoration purposes, it may be produced by mixing brown clay slip to the black stain. It will be obvious
to you that a much larger quantity of black stain is required to stain
a white clay. You may find when mixing some coloured stains to
slip that the mixture will not thicken; this is often the case with some
blue stains. To counteract this add a few drops of vinegar. The slip
may be made thinner again by simply adding a little water.

Percentage of stain to clay

The dealer's catalogue will advise of the amount of stain to be added to clay. Remember when the amount is stated as a percentage that this should be measured as dry weight. So, if 10 per cent. is recommended, this would mean ten parts of stain to one hundred parts of powder clay, or in metric terms ten grammes of stain to one hundred grammes of powder clay.

It is easy when using clay stains to judge the strength by looking at the colour when the ingredients are mixed. However, if oxides are used it is necessary to follow the instructions to the letter, since many oxides are in the form of black powder.

Glaze for decoration of coil pots

One of the methods suggested for the decoration of a coil pot was the application of oxide-stained transparent glazes to the incised markings made with a modelling tool. After the pot is dipped in tin glaze, or the glaze applied with a dabbing action using a brush loaded with the glaze, then each of the tool markings is painted with an oxide-stained glaze. This may be done in two ways. First a thin transparent glaze is stained with black copper oxide and then applied with a brush to each of the markings. The result is a terracotta pot showing glimpses of brown through the tin glaze covering and a diffused green-turquoise colour created by the mixing of tin and copper. Alternatively the colouring may be done with cobalt-stained glaze in a similar manner.

The oxide stains may be applied in alternate strokes to the markings: blue–green, blue–green. This may demand patience, but the result is worth the effort. In a later chapter there are other recipes and suggested glaze to colour proportions, but sometimes a simple measuring device such as a standard jam jar is suitable for mixing small amounts of glaze.

Example Recipe for application to tin-glazed terracotta coil pot.
Blue One level 5 ml spoon of black cobalt to a jar of transparent glaze.
Green One heaped 5 ml spoon to a jar of transparent glaze.

The glaze mixture for this decoration should be half strength, i.e. only half the normal amount of glaze powder should be added to the normal amount of water you use for dipping. Since the stained glaze is applied to the pot which has already been dipped, too thick a mixture would result in an overglazed pot.

Continuous coiling

There is a quick way of making a coil pot known as continuous coiling, or rope coiling. By using this method the pot may be built to a greater height more quickly than by any other coiling method. Cut a base to the size required by the design, and roll the clay thickly since it is to support a tall heavy pot. Your clay must be in a soft pliable condition to enable you to roll long ropes of clay without the risk of them cracking. Taper the end of the rope which is to be attached to the base, cross-hatch the base and paint with slip, then press the rope around the base. As the rope passes round it will override the beginning of the coil and produce the first step in the wall. This is usual and the step will appear all the way up the pot, to be corrected when the top limit is reached.

16 Putting on the first coil.   *17 Sealing the outside with thumb.*

For a successful strong pot it will be necessary to roll thick coils. With much practice it should be possible using 20 mm ($\frac{3}{4}$ in) clay coils to roll lengths of 50 cm (18 in) or more. As each loop is pressed, a widening process should emerge. Widen until the desired width

18 Sealing and smoothing the inside.   *19 Reaching the top.*

20 Trimming.   *21 Glaze pouring.*

22 Decorating with tin 'overglaze'

is reached, and then start to narrow the loops. The most important feature of this method is the sealing process. As each length is placed in position, sealing must follow immediately. Do not wait until you have completed building. Fig. 17 shows how one loop is smoothed into the next. These thumb markings may be left unsmoothed to form part of the decoration.

When the sealing of the loop is completed then the clay may be smoothed on the inside of the pot by the same method. The outside thumbing, and the inside smoothing of the pot will result in a finished vessel whose walls will now be approx. 12 mm ($\frac{1}{2}$ in) thick.

Materials and tools

The textured surface of the pot is ideal for glaze-dipped decoration. If as suggested earlier in the chapter the pot is dipped in tin glaze and the thumbed decoration rubbed slightly, the relief markings will show prominently against a milk-white background.

The use of a prepared Crystalline Chestnut glaze will also give excellent results. For the student wishing to experiment with glaze and colour a Zircon base glaze would provide an excellent background. Choose a matt, or semi-matt Zircon glaze, stain with 10 per cent. of copper oxide and add a sprinkling of dark rutile. Apply the glaze by dipping or pouring.

This type of decoration is particularly suitable if Staffordshire Red clay is used in making the pot.

Coil pot made with contrasting clays

It is possible to make coil pots with contrasting coloured clay coils, with this proviso—the clays must shrink at the same rate and by the same amount. One clay must not have more shrinkage than the other. Or, as with Agate clays, a white body could be stained to produce clays of different colours. I would recommend, however, that the two natural clays, Staffordshire Red and Buff School, are chosen for your first attempt. Make the pot in the usual way, but be sure to wash your hands after rolling each colour. Seal some of the coils; leave others in the coil shape to give you a pleasant design.

23 *Decorating selected coils.*

Slab Pottery

Whenever a piece of clay is flattened by hand, or rolled with a rolling pin, you have the beginnings of a slab pot. Many hand built models may be listed in this category. This chapter will include the simple clay models, rolled and cut around leaves and paper templates, and the more complicated cuboid and cylindrical shapes which provide the background for rich and exciting decoration.

Forming tiles, and pressings from plaster moulds has always been the main alternative to wheel pottery; it provides countless opportunities for the artist potter to produce variation in shape, and has led in modern times to the relatively new concept of ceramic sculpture. It has also brought a welcome change from the prolific production of wheel-thrown stoneware pottery, for many potters are now using stoneware techniques in the making of hand built pottery.

Here is a list of some items which can be made by slabbing:

The ceramic tile.
Tray with raised edges.
Pressed dish in plaster mould.
Tall vase made from slabs formed round a rolling pin or card tube.
Leaf shapes.
Slab formed on large sea or river pebble.
Cuboid and bottle shapes.
Mosaic panels.

There are many more examples of models made from slabbing, and all of them provide the potter with opportunities for inventive decoration.

We shall deal here with the skills and techniques of slabbing. Some of the items are quite simple, others are of a more complicated nature and require some measure of skill and patience.

Large cuboid pot

The making of a large slab pot demands more than manipulative skill. If the pot should crack in drying or firing, then all the time and effort in making is wasted. More important, though, is the great sense of disappointment to the potter in having failed. So care in selection and preparation of clay will be rewarded.

Leather-hard clay

You will have heard or read about the condition of clay in a leather-hard condition. A more correct term to describe this condition is soap-hard. This is when the clay can be cut or 'pared' with a knife as though cutting through soap. But, and it is important to note, this condition is too hard for the correct assembling and joining of the clay slabs. Since these are to be joined with slip, and sealed with soft clay, both slip and clay would dry too rapidly when in contact with the harder soap-hard clay.

The clay slabs must be sufficiently pliable so as to bend like cardboard, but without cracking in the process. When pressed with the fingers the clay should not resist the pressure.

Rolling

Using 10 mm ($\frac{3}{8}$ in) rolling guides, or 12 mm ($\frac{1}{2}$ in) if heavily grogged clay is selected, roll the clay to form slabs of 200×130 mm (8×5 in). You will need four pieces for the sides, and two pieces 130×130 mm (5×5 in) for base and top. These last two might be cut generously large to ensure a good fit when joined to the side. Sugar paper or linen-type material may be used as a base on which to roll the clay. In a warm classroom or kitchen these slabs would be ready for building in two to four hours time.

Tools

You will require a serrated edged tool for cross-hatching or 'scratching' the surfaces to be joined, a sharp knife for cutting, and a piece of wood of ruler length planed to 45° on one edge.

24 Cutting the slab. Note the guides which determine the thickness.

25 Slab must now be rolled between guides.

26 *Making a pattern with wooden block.*

27 *Roller pattern.*

28 *Pressed disc.*

29 *Cutting round the paper template.*

30 *Mitreing.*

31 *Cross-hatching the edges.*

Slip

Mix a thick clay slip from clay to be used for the pot. Use a large modelling board on which to build the pot.

Relief decoration

A cuboid pot made from grogged clay is an ideal medium for relief decoration, and this must be done whilst the clay is in a soft condition. There are many ways of effecting such decoration. For the first you need the services of an incised roller, easy to make from a piece of clay extruded from the pug-mill, or rolled into a cylinder shape by hand. This is incised using any object to suit your design. Scissor handles perform this task admirably. Fire the cylinder to biscuit and use it to roll along the surface of the slab. Secondly, try making some simple stamps or dies; these may be made in a roulette shape and fired to biscuit (see Fig. 28). Thirdly, cut a piece of wood long enough to accommodate the width of the slab. Cut some marquetry strip, and glue it on to the piece of wood. Then press this and tap it with a light hammer or rolling pin several times down the length of the clay slab.

It is not wise to measure and mark out the shapes of sides and base, but much better to use a paper or card template as this will ensure that all your pieces are of uniform size. Cut all the pieces slightly oversize so that when dried to the correct state they will not have shrunk below the original measurements. When ready cut them around the templates, and using the mitred ruler trim the edges of the four sides only to a 45° angle. Cross-hatch each of these mitred surfaces with the serrated tool. If this type of tool is not available you could use a pointed stick. Should there be any delay in building the pot when the clay is in the right condition, then the pieces should be placed in a plastic bag.

Assembly

Paint one edge of one side piece; lay flat on the board. Now repeat with the second piece. Lay the second piece mitre to mitre in position. The clay should be stiff enough to stand without support, but it would help if the two joined sides were laid against a wall surface for assisted support (see Fig. 33). When firmly stuck, place a sealing coil of soft clay in the corner formed by the two sides and model smoothly with finger tip or modelling stick. Repeat the process with the other two sides. There are now two 'L' shapes which when fixed together make the hollow box ready to place on the slab base.

The box may now be joined to the base, but first cross-hatch and paint the base with slip clay. Place the hollow box on the base, making sure that the sides are straight and not leaning inwards. The weight of the box will seal the base effectively, but added sealing coils between base and sides will make the joining even more secure.

If the pot is to be open ended for an intended vase shape it will be necessary to curve the top edges outwards slightly. The fingers should press gently on the top edge of each side and push outwards. A good example is the gently curved shape of a television screen. It must be stressed however that the pressure must be extremely gentle, moving the centre out no more than a fraction. As the pot dries and shrinks it is very likely that the top edges will dry quicker than the rest of the pot. This can lead to the edges curving inwards, putting a strain on the corners and spoiling the look of the pot. However, this example is intended to have a top with a trumpet opening, so the top may remain square. Make the trumpet shape well in advance so that it is stiff enough to handle—alternatively form the trumpet by thumbing the shape. Cut corresponding holes in the slab top and trumpet, and prepare to place the combination in position. Cross-hatch and paint with slip both pieces to be joined and when fixed pat all the outside edges firmly with a rolling guide stick. At the same time pat all the corner joinings even to the extent of making them rounded. If extra height is needed you could make a plinth to fit on the base. If this is attempted the plinth must be fitted before adding the trumpet to the top piece. It should be made as a box frame and fitted about 12 mm ($\frac{1}{2}$ in) inside the base. Allow the finished pot to dry slowly before firing.

Summary of method

1 **Cut paper templates for base and sides.**

2 **Choose thick rolling guides and roll slabs from grogged clay.**

3 **Decorate by incising with indent roller, roulette stamp, or strip stamp.**

4 **Cut slightly oversize around templates to allow for shrinkage. Dry to soap hard.**

5 **Now trim to size and mitre the sides only, to 45°. You will need to plane a wooden strip to obtain the 45° slope.**

32 Applying slip.

33 Joining two slabs, note the board supported by bricks.

34 Sealing the first half.

35 Sealing the second half.

36 Joining the two halves.

37 Sealing the remaining joints.

38 Beat the corners to make a permanent seal.

39 Placing the hollow box on base.

40 *Fitting the top.*

41 *Again beating the edges.*

42 *Clean up oversize edges with smoothing tool.*

43 *Putting on the trumpet top.*

44 *Glazing the finished pot.*

6 **Cross-hatch all surfaces to be joined.**

7 **Study Figs. 32–43 to observe the assembly: two sides supported by modelling board, or studio wall—seal corners—place two halves together—seal remaining corners—place on base slab—seal bottom and sides—cut hole in centre of top piece—make trumpet and fix in position using a generous amount of slip. The top should be tapped around the top edges to make a good joint.**

Finally, beat the mitred edges with a broad stick. Beat gently but firmly to make a permanent joint. If desired a plinth may be made to make the pot taller. This should be made and fixed when the pot is finished, and hardened enough for the plinth to support it.

Bottle shape slab pot

Using a grogged clay, either Buff or Staffordshire Red for an earthenware pot or a high firing clay for a stoneware pot, roll two large slabs and set aside to harden slightly. Your rolling guides to control the thickness of the clay should be not less than 10 mm (⅜ in) thick. 180 mm (7 in) diameter slab discs would be large enough for a first model. In fact, in practice you will find it necessary to reduce this, since the strip around the model would be very long and difficult to handle.

Whilst the disc slabs are hardening the long strip must be rolled, and it is sensible to roll two pieces to be joined by a mitre joint to the length required. The best approach to rolling this long strip,

45 *Rolling the strip.*

which one would expect to finish 50 mm (2 in) wide, is to form a thick coil of clay; place between rolling guides 75 mm (3 in) apart and roll. The guides should prevent your clay spreading more than necessary. A large drawing board covered with sugar paper provides a good base on which to roll slabs of clay, remembering of course that the paper should be replaced as it becomes saturated from constant rolling of damp clay.

Step by step instructions

1 **Join the two strips by mitreing. Paint the edges to be joined with clay slip.**

2 **Cut the strip oversize, allowing an overlay of an inch when mounting upon the first disc. Trim to required width.**

3 **Measure and mark a half way line on the strip, and cut a hole to accommodate the bottle top. Cut with the appropriate tile cutter.**

4 **The strip should now be bent into a circle whilst the clay is still soft, and left in this position until the placing and shaping process begins.**

46 *Joining two strips to make the required length.*

47 Strip placed and measured. Mark where the hole must be cut.

48 Cutting the hole.

49 Cutting the disc.

5 The large slab should now be sufficiently hard to handle, and should be placed on a wheel for cutting to size. This is easily done by holding a needle over the clay whilst the wheel is turning. Bring the needle slowly down until it makes contact with the clay, and press gently until the needle touches the wheel head. There must be no sudden 'jab', or the needle will travel to the centre of the wheel. The disc should be cut oversize at the first operation, and finally measured and cut, trimming to the correct size. If a wheel is not available, then a plate or a paper template could be used.

6 When both discs are cut, mark and cut an arc across the circumference of each of them. When formed with the strip in position the cutaway side of the finished cylinder will form the base of the pot.

7 The strip is placed around, but on 'top' of one of the discs. It is cut mitre fashion ready for joining, the joining being on the straight side of the pot, and in the centre. This puts the hole in the strip in its correct position at the top of the pot (opposite the joining).

50 Placing and joining strip to base.

51 Placing second side.   *52 Fitting the bottle top.*

8 Remove the strip, cross-hatch the edges and paint with slip.

9 Place the strip on top of the disc. The straight base edge may prove a little difficult, but the clay should be sufficiently pliable at this stage to follow the straightened edge of the circle.

10 Again cross-hatch the disc and paint with slip, and place the second disc in position. Pat the edge gently, but firmly, to ensure a permanent joint.

11 Make a wheel or thumb pot, cut a hole in its base, and place and seal over the hole at the top of the bottle (see Fig. 52).

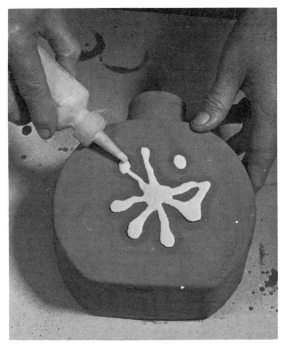

53 *Tin glaze trail pattern over pewter glaze.*

Slab pot around a rolling pin

This is a pot that has proved very popular with primary children, physically handicapped adults and patients recovering from mental illness. A common problem for students in these establishments is the lack of sophisticated equipment, and this model has been developed using only the minimum tools.

A large piece of grogged clay is required, and this is rolled into a slab between fairly thick rolling guides. Whilst still soft the clay is decorated with incised markings (see Fig. 54).

Choose a wide part of the slab and cut a straight edge. This edge will form the base. Now turn the clay over, put rolling pin into position and roll the clay around it. Lift the rolling pin and slab together, and start to seal. Where the edge overlaps seal into the body leaving thumb or finger marks for decoration. An extra precaution to help seal the edge is to paint the surfaces to be joined with slip.

54 Decorating rolled slab with roulette stamp.

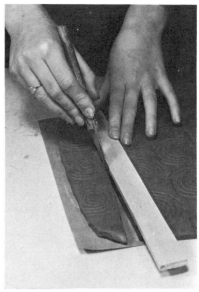

55 Trimming the bottom of the slab.

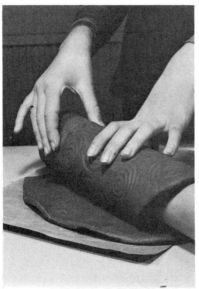

56 Rolling around the rolling pin.

57 Sealing.

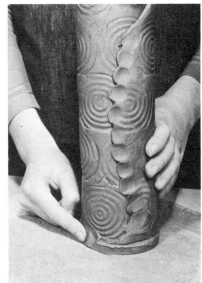

58 Placing on base.   *59 Sealing the base.*

It should be possible to stand the clay slab and rolling pin vertically whilst the base is cross-hatched and painted with slip. The 90 mm (3½ in) tile cutter shown on the left of Fig. 58 is exactly the right size to fit the pot. When the base is in position its oversize edge should be pulled up to seal it to the body.

The rolling pin is held in position whilst these operations are carried out. The pin needs to be pressed against the side of the tube (inside) to give support whilst sealing. However, it must be removed gently when the base is in position. If left too long it could prove difficult to remove.

Decoration

The type of decoration for this tall pot immediately comes to mind. Since the whole area is covered with incised markings a coloured or matt white glaze would suit it admirably. If the pot is dipped or rolled in a white matt glaze, the markings could be rubbed with the fingers, and when fired a little of the clay colour would break through

60 Glaze dipping. The pot is rolled over in the glaze.

the glaze. Or a Rockingham brown glaze would give a depth of colour which would suit the shape.

The method of glazing is simple. Just pour the glaze into a bowl, about the size of a washing-up bowl, and roll the pot over and over until completely covered with glaze.

Slab pot round a cardboard tube

This is a simple method of making a round vessel comparable with one made on the wheel, and can be a reasonable alternative if wheel pottery is not practised. A short piece of card tube is required, about 100 mm (4 in) wide, and this is covered with polythene sheeting. When fastened with sticky tape the clay slab may be wrapped around the tube without fear of it sticking.

A paper template is cut and measured round the tube; then the clay is rolled, allowed to dry a little so that it is easy to handle, and after cutting, using the paper template for accuracy, measured around the tube for final cutting and placing.

The slab is then marked, cut with mitred edges, cross-hatched, painted with slip and joined.

The base is made slightly oversize, and the spare clay used for extra sealing. A lid may now be rolled and cut, and a lip formed from a coil of clay. Fig. 63 shows how the coil is formed and smoothed using a notched stick.

61 Joining the mitred strip.

62 Placing on base.

63 Forming the lid.

Leaf model

A sycamore leaf provides a pleasant shape for a pottery wall-plaque or small tray. It is possible to pick leaves in late September and seal them in a plastic bag to use in the winter. Of course early summer is the ideal time when young trees grow leaves the size of dinner plates. To make a tray, either buff or white clay, according to the decoration envisaged, is rolled between rolling guides. The leaf is placed on the clay slab, and pressed gently with a rolling pin. This pressure ensures that the veins at the back of the leaf are pressed into the clay thereby creating a perfect incised copy of the front of the leaf. Experience has shown that the most efficient way

64 Pricking out the shape.   *65 'Pulling' the edges.*

to cut round the leaf is by using a cocktail-stick. The plastic or wooden stick is pointed, and when pressed into the clay at very close intervals it enables you to 'drag' the clay away, leaving a serrated edge.

When teaching young children or the handicapped a stick proves safer than a sharp knife. Children particularly love to make the 'stitch' marks, and the results are always satisfying. When the leaf shape is cut the edges should be curved slightly. Do not turn a 'pie-crust' edge, but curve gently upwards.

Decoration

The leaf may be glaze-decorated in several ways when biscuit fired.

1 **The first and obvious decoration is by dipping into a fairly dark green glaze. Copper oxide mixed with a transparent glaze is exactly the right colour. If stains are used or coloured glazes, then a grass green would be fine.**
2 **Dip or paint the leaf with Crystalline Chestnut glaze. Now**

66 Raising the sides.

*67 Cystalline chestnut
and yellow for an
Autumn leaf.*

mix a little bright yellow glaze, and with a brush dab the
edges. Paint from the outside edge to the centre, but
diminish the amount of glaze as you reach the centre. Fire at
the recommended temperature; for earthenware around
1060°C.

3 Draw a pencil line at a distance and parallel to the outside
of the leaf shape. Paint the centre up to the line with a thick
layer of Blood Red glaze. Use the dabbing action with a hog-
hair brush, and dab layer upon layer to deposit glaze to a
depth of 3mm ($\frac{1}{8}$in). Now apply Gold Lustre glaze again
almost as thickly to the border of the leaf, leaving the back
unglazed except for a narrow border on the upturned curve.

68 This model is being painted with Blood Red and gold lustre.

Slab fish

One model which is simple to make and decorate and gives immediate success is the slab fish. First roll the clay, cut it into a fish shape using a paper template and then, using finger and thumb moistened with water, smooth and lift the edges into a gentle curve. Below is a table of glazes you can use.

1 **Brown clay with incise markings (see Fig. 69). Dip in tin glaze, and brush copper oxide glaze on each marking. Or mix a turquoise glaze by adding copper to tin glaze, and dip the model (at the biscuit stage of course). Fire at 1060°C.**

Now make several fish without the incise markings from white or brown clay, and decorate in the following manner.

2 **Dip in Crystalline Chestnut glaze, and spot, using a bottle slip trailer, with tin glaze.**

3 **Dip in cobalt glaze, and spot with tin glaze.**

4 **Dip in copper glaze and spot with tin glaze.**

There are many powerful glazes from which to choose, which will react dramatically when the tin glaze melts and picks up the colour beneath. Fire between the range 1060°C. and 1080°C.

69 Incised markings.

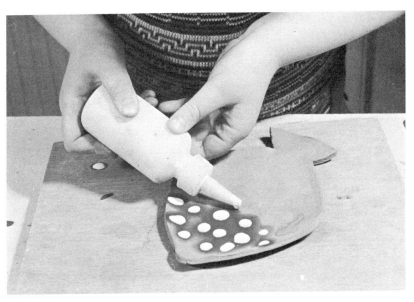

70 Glaze spotting.

Wheel Pottery

It must be understood at the outset that the potter must be the master of the wheel—controlling the speed of the wheel for the various operations, and exerting considerable pressure upon the clay to force it into the correct positions. You will realize, of course, that centrifugal force is at work all the time, trying as it were to throw the clay off the spinning wheel. Whether it stays on depends upon two factors: the plastic condition of the clay and the pressure and direction of the potter's hands. Only practice, lots and lots of practice, will ensure success for the beginner.

Clay preparation

If the clay you are using comes directly from a new supply then little preparation is required, for it will come from the clay merchant pugged and de-aired. In this case patting into a ball is all that is necessary. If, however, the clay has been used previously and comes from your own pugmill or clay bin, then more care is needed before attempting to throw. You should first ensure that the clay is sufficiently plastic and if not, add water by pancaking, i.e. flatten the clay into a cake, add water, fold over and knead. When this is done wedge the clay well by throwing on a firm bench, cut through with a wire-cutter and examine for the presence of air holes. Join the opposite ends and wedge again.

Weigh a lump of clay about 1.4 kg (3 lbs) and throw or slap the clay hard upon the wheel endeavouring to hit the centre. If the clay is excessively off-centre then push and pull into position.

The wheel has not yet turned so look around to see that all your preparations are complete—bowl of water on the tray, a bowl or bucket in position beneath the waste hole, and finally a needle for trimming, and a wire for cutting the pot from the wheel. Later, when you intend firing your work, you will require turning tools for turning the base. Also have a sponge floating in the bowl of water ready for use.

71 *Pressing the lump in centre of wheel.*

Throwing technique

The first operation is known as centreing and your wheel must be turning at its fastest speed. Put both wet hands around the clay, allowing the fingers of the left hand to overlap those of the right, brace the forearms on the wheel edge, and try to pull the clay towards you. If the clay is off-centre it will tend to push your hands away, so considerable pressure will be required to pull it towards the centre of the wheel. When this is done interlock your fingers and squeeze the clay until it begins to grow. You may already require more water on your hands. Dry hands cause friction, and friction will result in the clay breaking off from the wheel head.

When the clay has grown to cone shape put your thumbs together, and with fingers clasping the clay, press downwards. The thumbs will finally press the clay into a solid cylindrical shape. When these movements have been repeated several times the clay should be sufficiently wedged to allow your next operation to continue. This is to form a cylinder 100 mm (4 in) across and 75 mm (3 in) high. Put the left palm on the centre of the cylinder, with fingers of the right hand supporting the right side, and press downwards; finally slide the left hand slowly across and off. Now smooth from base to top with the fingers of the right hand.

Your may find that the cylinder requires re-centreing and this must be done carefully. Take up the original centreing position; pull towards you, sliding the fingers up and over the clay slowly. Remember, never take your hands away abruptly.

Figs. 75 to 80 are self explanatory and explain how the pot may be opened, widened and narrowed.

72 *Centring.*

73 *Wedging.*

74 *Forming the cylinder.*

75 *Thumbing the centre hole.*

76 *Widening.*

77 *Pinching up.*

78 'Pinching' making the pot 'Grow'.

79 'Knuckling up' and 'Bulging'.

80 Narrowing the neck.

81 Shaping the pouring spout.

82 *Pouring spout completed.*

83 *A cylinder shape cut in half. Notice the clay thickness.*

84 *Finger position for 'bulging'.*

85 *Finger position for narrowing.*

Cutting off

It is not very difficult to remove a narrow pot from the wheel, although of course great care must be taken. Special cutting wire is obtainable from the pottery dealers, and may be looped at the ends, or have short wooden handles to grip. Pass the wire underneath the pot as near to the wheel head as possible and, without delay, with thumbs at the front and fingers behind the pot, tilt forward and lift. If a large heavy pot has been thrown then the wrists must be pressed closely together, still with fingers and thumbs in position, and the extra pressure should lift off the pot.

A much simpler and safer way for beginners is to slide the pot from the wheel head. Pass the wire underneath the pot, splash water on the wheel around the pot and cut again. You may now see the pot move. When this happens, hold a wet board level with the wheel head and slide the pot on to it. Your movements at this stage must be very gentle. Experienced potters will lift off the pot after cutting once, but this calls for great dexterity in handling, and will take some time to achieve. If after cutting and sprinkling with water the pot does not move a sure way to get it to slide is to pass a second, thicker wire under the pot. This will move the pot quickly and efficiently.

Turning

It is possible to turn a pot in much the same way as an engineer turns a piece of metal on a lathe and in fact lathes are used in the pottery industry. You will of course use your wheel for this operation, and you must wait until your pot is soap-hard before attempting to turn the pot.

Some potters prefer to finish their pots at the making stage, especially in the case of jugs when a handle would prevent the potter using a turning tool. If you wish to do this you should turn some of the thick clay from the base of the pot, and use a kidney rubber to smooth the outside surface.

On the other hand you may prefer to keep the base and walls fairly thick so that some of the clay may be turned off and a foot formed at the base. As mentioned earlier, the pot must be in soap-hard condition so that the clay is easily turned off with the turning tool. The pot must be secured to the wheel head so that it will not be flung off when the wheel begins to turn. You may use one of two methods. One is to wet the wheel slightly and move the pot vigorously until it begins to stick, then move it quickly into the centre of the wheel so that it is centred. Another safety factor used by many potters is to press three pieces of clay around the pot, securing the pot to the wheel.

When you are ready to start turn the wheel slowly, hold your finger against the rim of the pot, and check that the pot is centred. If not, it must be adjusted or the turning tool will take more clay from one side of the pot, leaving the other side thin and weak. Another check is to pass a needle through the side of the pot to check the thickness. As a beginner you might also check the base of the pot to ensure that it is thick enough to turn a foot. A thin base on a pot will develop a cobweb of cracks when drying and shrinking from the walls. If the base is thin it is safer to level the base only, taking the minimum amount of clay off with a tool or wooden ruler.

Although turning tools of many shapes are available from the pottery dealers it is possible to make your own, and many experienced potters prefer to do this. Old, used saw blades may be ground and bent into turning tools. They must be ground so that the cutting edge is sharp and smooth, however, as rough edges would leave a trail of scratch marks on the pot. Therefore, after grinding, the tool should be finally smoothed on an oil stone and bent at the angle required.

Points to remember

1 **Centreing and wedging: brace arms on wheel-edge.**

2 **Opening up: press the thumb to within 17 mm ($\frac{5}{8}$ in) from the base. Insert fingers of the left hand and thumb of the right hand.**

3 **If an air bubble appears, cut it open and press some soft clay in the hole.**

4 **Wheel must be turning quickly when centreing, slowly when turning.**

5 **Do not use too much pressure when knuckling-up.**

6 **Do not use too much pressure when 'bulging'.**

7 **Do not try to make a pot with a fast moving wheel.**

8 **Do not be in a hurry.**

9 **When turning delicate pieces such as a candle holder, the left hand should be placed around the pot, not holding it but in a position to grasp should the pot move.**

Pulling a handle

A large jug demands a stout handle so make sure that your handle is strong and large enough to be efficient in use. The best handle is the pulled handle. The clay must be soft and well wedged, and may first be rolled into a cylinder shape. Holding the shape over a bowl of water or a wash basin, grasp one end firmly in one hand and with the other stroke the shape gently in a downward direction.

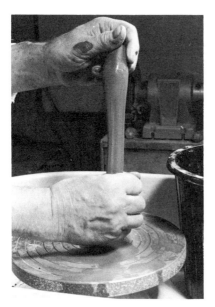

86 Pulling a handle.

87 Pressing the handle opposite the spout.

The stroking hand must be wet all the time otherwise the friction caused will break off the clay piece by piece. The handle will assume the space between your first finger and thumb, and if it appears slightly ridged this should be left as part of the decorative effect. You should try to pull a 'flat' on the inside of the handle, both for ease of bending and for grasping when the finished pot is in use.

When the shape is long enough, and you consider thin enough, or of the right thickness, it should be measured against the side of the pot and cut. Slice the top of the handle at an angle where it is to fit the top of the pot, and secure with clay slip.

88 *Sealing the handle.*

89 *Pinching up the honey jar shape.*

Making a honey jar

The honey jar with lid is modelled on the idea of the old pottery bread bin. Older people may remember the tall terracotta vessel with looped handles at the sides, glazed only on the inside and partly on the outside, leaving roughly two thirds of the outside unglazed. Figs. 101 and 102 show the handles being fixed, and Figs. 98 and 99 show the lid being turned. It is advisable to leave the jar to go leather-hard before fixing the handles which should be a little softer than the jar. When the handles have been firmly secured the top third of the jar may be dipped in black slip. It is not intended to leave any part unglazed, so when the pot is biscuit fired it should be dipped in transparent glaze and fired at 1060°C.–1070°C.

Lids may be made in two ways. The first is the simplest, and should not present any problems (see Fig. 98). The second needs to be a more accurate fit and requires a lip to be made at the top of the jar for it to rest upon (see Fig. 91). This lip is made before the thrown clay becomes too thin when 'knuckling' up. You can use a modelling stick, pressing the point into the thick rim, and then turning the clay inwards to form the lip. When the lip is formed and the pot thrown to size, measure across the top to determine the size of the lid. It is essential that both lid and jar will be the same so the lid should be a good fit in the jar. You must allow both to dry separately, and constantly make checks to see that the lid has not become too tight. If this happens rub the edge with steel wool or sandpaper.

90 Flattening and
thickening the top.

91 Incising the lip with
wooden tool.

92 Turning and flattening.

93 Final shaping.

94 Cutting off.

95 Lifting off.

96 *Turning the foot.*

97 *Finished foot.*

98 *Turning the lid.*

99 *Turning to fit the jar.*

100 *Lid fitting the jar.*

101 *Cross-hatching for handle.*

102 *Fitting one handle.*

103 *Finished pot with alternative lid fitting.*

104 *Dipping jar into black slip.*

105 *Note depth of slip. Finished jar is shown in Fig. 103.*

Making a candle holder

Whilst students are becoming efficient on the wheel it builds their confidence to have some success. So here is a fairly simple wheel pot to make; 0·2 kg (½ lb) of buff or white clay would make the pot, and provide the base for a pleasant decoration.

Wedge and centre the clay into a cone shape. Choose a position near the base of the cone, and mark with one finger, applying slight pressure to make a groove. The wheel must not turn too quickly for any of the techniques involved.

Turn your attention to the top of the cone. Thumb a hole as shown in earlier wheel instructions. Press down until your thumb is within 12 mm (½ in) of the bottom and form the shape as shown in Fig. 107.

The holder shape starts from the groove previously made and when the shape is complete you should form the base. When making the hole to accommodate the candle it will be necessary to make it slightly larger than the candle to allow for shrinkage. This is perhaps an awkward shape to cut from the wheel, and it may be necessary

Plate 1 Hand-built stoneware
pot, known as the
'Provence' pot.
Overglaze decoration.

Plate 2 Hand-built stoneware
pot. Note the top at
right-angles to the
sides.

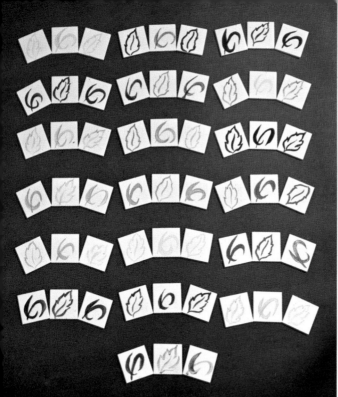

Plate 3 Underglaze colours

Plate 4 On-glaze colours.

Plate 5 Clay body stains.

Plate 6 Lead-free earthenware
    glazes.

Plate 7 Taggs Yard stoneware glazes.

Plate 8 Stoneware glazes. Oxidising and reducing.

Plate 9 Low solubility earthenware artistic glazes.

Plate 10 Stoneware oxidising glazes.

Plate 11 Clown. Glaze
decoration.

Plate 12 Clown. Glaze
decoration.

Plate 13 Ceramic jewellery.

Plate 14
Collection of wheel
pots with various
decorative techniques.

15 Slip trailed plaques.

Plate 16 Leaf and fish shapes.
Coloured and tin glaze
decoration.

Plate 17 Mosaic shapes.

Plate 18 Mosaic shapes.

Plate 19 Mosaic.

to wet the wheel head and slide the pot on to a wet board. First slide a wire under the pot, having splashed water liberally on the wheel head, wet a board and put in position on the edge and level with the wheel head. Now slide the pot on to the board. If it does not move easily, slide a twisted wire beneath and this will move the pot quickly.

When the candle holder is leather-hard you may wish to turn the sides to provide a smooth surface. When turning the base you must have your fingers around the pot. This is because the narrow top is not very secure and could move. If it does move the hand may grasp it easily to prevent it leaving the wheel.

To make the handle you should roll a small coil and flatten it by pressing with a flat stick. Dampen with a few strokes from a wet hand, measure, and bend into the handle shape. Leave it for a little while so that it becomes slightly stiffer and thereby easier to handle. In time you will have the skill and confidence to fix the handle whilst it is still in a soft state.

*106 Ridging the base from
cone shape.*

107 Thumbing the hole.

108 Shaping the 'stick'.

109 Narrowing for candlestick lip.

110 Finishing touches.

111 Cleaning up the base with turning tool.

112 Turning the foot.

113 Fixing a handle.

114 Glaze dipping.

115 Finished models.

Decoration

The decoration shown in Fig. 115 is obtained by dipping the candle holder into a Pewter glaze. This is particularly suitable if you have made a pot with a wide base, and a short holder. When glost fired this model has a metallic finish which looks rather like the old fashioned pewter candlestick.

If the model has a narrow base and the stick is tall, then there is a very handsome decorative finish you might try. You will require a satin-matt glaze and one of the many coloured glazes available. The matt glaze is poured into the top of the holder, which is then held upside down, and dipped a little below the rim in the same white matt glaze. Using a coloured glaze dip the rest of the pot up to the white glaze and glost fire. Apollo, copper green, chestnut or pewter, are just a few decorative glazes you might use in contrast to the white glaze.

116 Collection of wheel pots.

Glazes & Glazing

'Modern glazes are mixtures of complex silicates and borates. They are compounded in order to produce a covering for ceramic bodies which shall be among other things:

1 **Insoluble in water and the usual acids and alkalis likely to be met in use.**

2 **Resistant to scratching.**

3 **As far as possible impervious.**

4 **Resistant to crazing, peeling and similar faults.**

5 **Suitable for producing certain decorative effects, such as colour, crystal development etc.**

6 **Fusible at predetermined temperature ranges.'**

(Ceramic Glazes—Borax Consolidated Ltd.)

This is a simple and fair assessment of what a glaze is, and what it must do. It only remains now to interpret the technical data of ceramic experts. Glaze is glass! If we substitute silica for sheet glass, add red lead for a fluxing agent and china clay in small amounts to check the flow of molten glazes, then we have a very efficient transparent glaze. This mixture is known as a glaze-frit. This is an important term, in an important pottery process.

If you understand glazes and the effects of glaze upon clay your success as a potter is assured, for how often have you seen beautifully modelled pots and thrown ware ruined by inferior decoration or inadequate glazing? This is so often the failing of the beginner, and understandably so. It leads to early disappointment just when success is needed. If the work of children or adult students is spoiled by inferior glazing, their long faces will tell you of your failure as a teacher.

Glaze constituents

First and foremost in studying glazes and their application, you should know what a glaze contains, and possibly know the purpose of some of the constituents. You must remember that a fired pot is extremely porous and when dipped in a liquid will accept water and soluble materials. For instance, if you dissolve sugar with water the sugar with the water would be absorbed by the pot. By the same rule glaze constituents which are soluble would also be absorbed and would not, therefore, perform the function of covering the surface of the pot with a layer of glaze.

So, the glaze materials must be made insoluble. This process is called 'fritting'. A typical glaze frit to produce a transparent glaze would be made from the following: red lead 65 per cent., silica 32 per cent., china clay 3 per cent., and would be known when fritted as lead-basilicate. A 'Podmore' transparent glaze would be made from borax frit 70 per cent., lead frit 25 per cent. and china clay 5 per cent. A 'Podmore' stoneware glaze would be made up of the following: feldspar 26 per cent., whiting 18.5 per cent., barium carbonate 2.5 per cent., quartz 38 per cent., and china clay 15 per cent. A non-lead frit is produced when the lead flux is substituted by borax.

Fritting

The frit materials lead, silica and china clay, or borax, silica and china clay are fired in special ovens and when the temperature reaches 1100°C., the whole mass is dropped in water where it shatters and breaks into small nuggets; in the case of the lead frit the colour of the nuggets is golden yellow, while the borax frit pieces are a delicate purplish blue. These small pieces are then ground in a ball mill, where a hard grinding media revolving in the mill grinds the brittle frit into a white powder. This powder is nearly 100 per cent.

insoluble. It is important to remember that the borax and the lead constituents are never fritted together. The reason for this is that the borax would render the lead frit soluble, and the really important aspect of fritting is to render the materials insoluble—first for successful glazing, so that the water in the glaze will sink into the porous pot and the glaze powder will remain on the surface of the pot—and second to protect the health of the potter, since absorption of the lead content into the bloodstream would be harmful.

These frits are stored by the manufacturers until supplies of specialist glazes are needed, such as transparent, matt and opaque glazes etc., then other ingredients are added to produce the various earthenware and stoneware glazes. Typical recipes for these are included in the following pages.

Classification of glazes

Glazes may be classified as follows:

1 Lead containing

2 Leadless

3 Based on the ware to which it is applied
(a) Majolica
(b) Earthenware
(c) Sanitary
(d) Porcelain

4 Based on the effect produced on the finished article
(a) Transparent
(b) Opaque
(c) Matt
(d) Semi-matt
(e) Satin Vellum

5 Based on temperature
(a) Majolica 900°C.–1050°C. ⎫ Fritted glazes
(b) Earthenware 1000°C.–1150°C. ⎭
(c) Stoneware 1200°C.–1300°C. ⎫ Raw glazes
(d) Porcelain over 1300°C. ⎭

Glaze recipes

Transparent glazes

Mention has already been made of the materials which go into producing transparent glazes. These are basically clear glasses which allow the pottery body to show through. They are suitable for underglaze decoration and glaze staining, and one will always obtain brighter glazes and obtain better colour development when lead is present in the glaze.

Opaque glazes

This type of glaze can be produced in two ways:

(a) By adding an opacifier such as tin oxide or zircon (zirconium silicate) to a Transparent Glaze.
(b) By using an opacified frit (borax and zircon). This frit ('Podmore') plus 5 per cent. of china clay will produce a good white opaque glaze at 1060°C.

Recipe

1040°C.–1100°C.		1200°C.–1300°C.	
(a) White opaque zircon frit	95%	(c) Feldspar	34%
China clay	5%	Whiting	12%
		Barium carbonate	5%
(b) Borax frit	65%	Zinc oxide	3%
Tin oxide	7%	China clay	8%
Zinc oxide	14%	Disperzon	14%
China clay	14%	Quartz	24%

Opacifiers such as tin oxide or zirconium silicate (Disperzon) have a refractive index higher than the base glaze and therefore have the ability to bend the light by reflection and refraction. The finer the particle size of the opacifier the greater is the opacity produced.

Matt glazes

Matt glazes differ from transparent glazes in having a mass of tiny crystals embedded in a glassy matrix. They are formed when a completely fused glass cools and part of it crystallizes out. The crystallization is promoted by cooling whilst the glaze is still in its molten form, e.g. earthenware range having maximum temperature at 1060°C. and slow cooling between 1060°C. and 800°C. will promote crystallization. All matt glazes should therefore be cooled slowly for best results.

The Vellum matt glaze has a much smaller crystal size than the standard matt glaze and is much smoother to touch. The Vellum-type glazes are usually composed of low solubility lead glazes with combinations of tin-oxide, titanium dioxide and zinc oxide.

It is possible to take a standard transparent glaze and by additions convert to firstly an Opaque glaze and then into a Matt glaze. The following is an example:

Transparent glaze

Borax frit	70 parts by weight
Lead frit	25 parts by weight
China clay	5 parts by weight

To convert the above into a glossy opaque glaze add 5 parts of tin oxide or 5 parts of Disperzon (zirconium silicate).

To convert the opaque glossy glaze into a matt glaze add 18 parts of zinc oxide and 4 parts of titanium dioxide.

Recipe for matt and vellum glazes
1040°C.–1100°C.

Lime Matt		*Satin Vellum*	
Lead bisilicate	17%	Lead bisilicate	50%
Borax frit	43%	Borax frit	20%
Feldspar	18%	Zircon	12%
Quartz	4%	Titania	3%
China clay	5%	Tin oxide	3%
Whiting	13%	Zinc oxide	6%
		China clay	6%

Stoneware matt white
1200°C.–1300°C.

Feldspar	32%
Whiting	12%
Barium carbonate	5%
Zinc oxide	3%
China clay	9%
Disperzon	17%
Quartz	22%

Glaze mixing and application

Before mixing your glaze consider whether you will require a suspender or glaze-binder for your mixing. A suspender (bentonite or calcium chloride) is used to keep the glaze in suspension whilst glazing. A glaze-binder gives increased strength to unfired glazes and helps to minimize flaking or chipping the glaze before firing. These would be used mainly in industry where large amounts of glaze are mixed and large numbers of pots are to be glazed. School and hobby potters rely on stirring and re-sieving the glazes which have settled in the bottom of containers.

Half a kg (1 lb) of glaze powder to about half a litre (1 pint) of water is roughly the ratio for a start. This will give you a 'wet' glaze. However, if you have time allow the glaze to settle so that the water rises to the top and then decant and mix the glaze to the consistency to suit your fired ware. This consistency will be decided by the porosity of the pot. Test this by putting the tip of your tongue to the pot. If a low fired pot, then your tongue will stick to the pot. If a high fired pot, then the mark of your saliva will show. Therefore if the pot is porous your glaze must be 'thin'. The porous pot will accept a lot of the water in the glaze and leave a generous amount of glaze powder adhering to the biscuitware. If the pot is vitreous (high fired) then the glaze must be mixed thickly. A thin glaze over a highly fired pot would result in a very thin covering of glaze and when fired the pot would probably be bare of glaze in places.

You can apply the glaze by dipping, pouring, spraying or brushing. The aim is to obtain a good even coating all over, and this is most easily achieved by dipping. If sufficient glaze is mixed, or the pots are small, you may be able to immerse them completely. In this case the pot should be held by the tips of the fingers, and you might first touch these places with a little glaze before dipping so that it will not be bare of glaze when the pot is removed from the bucket. Now, immerse completely, count three seconds and then remove. Hold the pot until the glaze has dried, which will be very rapid if the pot is low fired. Check whether your fingers have left marks on the pot and retouch with a little glaze if necessary.

Before placing in the kiln wipe the glaze from the foot of the pot to prevent the molten glaze from adhering to the kiln batt; an extra precaution is to place the pot on a stilt. A good test to determine the correct thickness of the glaze is to scrape through the glaze layer with your thumb nail. If the thickness of the glaze is shown as thick as newspaper then you have the right amount of glaze on the pot. Many school and hobby potters keep a stock of small tiles made from various clays and fired at predetermined temperatures so that they may use them as test pieces for both glazing and firing.

Another way of putting an even layer of glaze on the pot when only a small amount of glaze has been mixed is to pour and dip. A hollow vessel such as a beaker or jug would have glaze poured into it, then the pot would be lowered into the glaze whilst holding it by the foot. This may be difficult to do if the pot has been fired too high, for when the pot has absorbed water from the glaze on the inside it may be too wet to hold glaze on the outside. So, perhaps the golden rule of firing and glazing is to 'fire the pot low at the biscuit stage, and high at the glost stage'. This might be opposite to industrial firing, but will ensure certain success by beginners.

Another way of dipping when only small amounts of glaze are mixed is again to pour glaze into the pot and then to dip in two movements; dip from the bottom to half way, then invert the pot and dip the other half.

Spraying

Glaze spraying can present problems. In the first place it is really necessary to have some kind of spraying booth, whether it be home made or professionally made. The pot should be placed in a spray booth and ideally an extractor motor should be used so that glaze in the atmosphere is not inhaled. When spraying, care should be taken to see that every part of the pot receives the same amount of glaze, otherwise the glazing will be patchy.

Glaze painting

There is a danger that in glaze painting large, thick amounts of glaze on the sides of pots will melt and run on to the kiln batts. The painting process is better suited to flat slabware and figures where several shades of colour are necessary. For instance there is no better way of decorating the leaf pot than by painting. It must be remembered though that ordinary brush strokes will not suffice. They will appear streaky when fired. The glaze must be applied with a dabbing action, each 'dab' meeting the next for complete coverage.

The leaf pot illustrated in Fig. 67 has been decorated to copy the browns and yellows of an autumn leaf. First the leaf was dabbed all over with a Crystalline Chestnut glaze, then the edges were dabbed lightly with an intense yellow glaze and the centre with still lighter strokes. When fired the pottery leaf takes on the colours of autumn when the yellow glazes mingle and are diffused into the chestnut background.

The glaze painting of figures is an alternative process to the underglaze painting method. Underglaze painting is difficult for young and old alike, but if coloured glazes are properly controlled and applied the finished decoration can be dramatically beautiful. The biscuit figure should be damped slightly so that there is not too thick a build up of glaze. The coloured glazes should be mixed thinly, and the colours dabbed on with a hog hair brush.

Points to remember

1 Keep glaze covered when not in use.

2 Replace water content if glaze has been standing for a long time. Make test dippings for safety.

3 Check the porosity of your pots. Touch the biscuit pot with the tip of your tongue. Your tongue will stick slightly if the pot is porous; in this case add more water to the glaze.

4 Thick glaze for highly fired pots.

5 Wipe the base of a glazed pot on a piece of wet felt before placing in kiln, or place ware on stilts. Grind stilt points off the base after firing.

6 If you anticipate a high firing of a low temperature lead glaze, or if by experience you have found that the glaze 'runs' and beads on the base of the pots, add a small amount of china clay to your glaze.

7 Undissolved oxides stirred loosely in the glaze will provide speckled effects—more effective in opaque or matt glazes.

8 A matt glaze must be cooled slowly after firing, especially between maturing temperature and 800°C.

9 What to do with your glaze remains. Do not wash these away down the sink. Have a bin or container handy, and put all these scraps of glaze into it. When there is sufficient to make a mixing, put through a 40s sieve so that the ingredients are not too finely mixed. Use as a background decoration for tin glaze, or for an addition of rutile. An interesting decoration is possible on tiles and slabware. Dip the article in the glaze, then drop thick spots of tin glaze on the surface; the tin will melt and spread, picking up the colours in the glaze beneath.

10 Keep all utensils such as buckets and sieves clean when mixing and, if possible, keep a glaze sieve specially for white glazes. Once cobalt is put through a sieve there is always a chance that specks of it will appear on all your glazing.

Slip Cast Pottery

This is an industrial mass production method of making pots, and consequently often under criticism by some art-potters. Others realize the value of learning a complete industrial process, and then turning it to their own use to produce a finished article which gives joy to teacher and student alike.

By this method you are able to make vessels of thin clay which do not have to be hollowed out to fire safely. With practice you will master many intricate mould-making techniques, and with many plaster casts available to you, will be able to try the technical decorative processes which give the models a professional look.

Specially mixed liquid clay is poured into a plaster mould. The liquid is allowed to stay in the mould for ten minutes or so according to the dry state of the plaster. Whilst the clay slip is in the mould the plaster absorbs the water from it.

In a one-piece mould you can note the thickening of solid clay around the edges. This thickness may determine when the remaining liquid shall be poured back into the slip bucket. If not thick enough, and the level of the slip is lowering you may 'top-up' with more slip.

When the mould is emptied, a hollow clay shape remains rather like a clay shell. This must remain in the mould until dry, when a tap on the bottom of the mould will bring out the vessel cleanly. It should now stand on a flat surface and be fettled with knife and sponge. If there is any doubt as to when the pot should be removed from the mould, a certain way to judge is to wait until the wet shine has left the clay. This can be observed fully only with a one-piece mould. However a check on the pouring neck of two- or multi-piece moulds will give you some indication of its state; simply slice off a small piece from the neck of the pouring hole after an interval of half an hour or more.

Clay for slip-casting

Liquid clay for slip-casting is known as deflocculated clay, and some knowledge of the alkali sodium silicate is necessary. All potters know that an ordinary mixing for slip trailing demands about half a litre (1 pt) of water to half a kg (1 lb) of powder clay. So it may be surprising to learn that your mixing of 9 kg (20 lb) of clay powder must use only 4 litres (7½ pt) of water. If a normal mixing of slip were used, the plaster would quickly become saturated and would not perform the task of absorbing sufficient water to allow a thick deposit of clay to build up on the plaster wall.

Here is the recipe:

9 kg (20 lb) of powder clay
4 litres (7½ pt) of water
28 g (1 oz) silicate of soda (140 TW) (TW—degrees of density)
28 g (1 oz) soda ash (added to give strength to the clay vessel)

Dissolve the thick silicate of soda in a little hot water and add the soda ash. When thoroughly dissolved, add the powder clay by sprinkling and stirring. Remember the clay must be weighed carefully. When mixed, the thick sticky liquid should be brushed through a 40s sieve. Do this at least twice and leave to stand for several hours before using.

Clay is composed of minute flakes of clay which move and slide over each other according to the water content. The introduction of these two materials, both alkalines, allows this to happen with the minimum water content. Technically these substances which make deflocculation possible are called electrolytes.

Points to remember

1 **The mould absorbs a lot of water each time a cast is poured, so more time may be required to cast subsequent models.**

2 **When the mould is emptied the clay begins to shrink. Loosen any portion which appears to be sticking.**

3 **Do not attempt to remove the cast too soon or it will collapse.**

4 **When making two or multi-piece moulds, take care with the joints; the model is neater if the casting seams are not too obvious.**

5 **Slip which has been standing for some time should be passed through a sieve; this helps to liquefy any clay beginning to skin or harden.**

Making the mould

Pattern making

Industry would use either clay or plaster for making patterns to be used in mould making. Clay would be used for modelling patterns of animals, human figures, birds etc.; and in some cases where there were protuberances of arms or legs, these would be cut from the figure and separate moulds made for them. The casts from all these moulds would then be assembled, and fixed firmly with slip at the leather-hard stage of the clay. For domestic earthenware and china, plaster patterns would be used to produce moulds for cups, basins, plates etc.

There are differing methods of using these moulds of course; for plates, saucers and cups and many other hollow vessels a machine known as a Jigger and Jolley would be used.

The craft of mould-making is complex, and workers require long training to acquire the necessary skills to produce working moulds. Before these working moulds can be made, a block and case must be made so that subsequent moulds can be produced from the original.

First, a mould is made from the pattern, and it is from this that a block and case is made. Wherever the plaster surfaces make contact they are brushed with 'potter's size' for easy separation. This is a solution of soft soap diluted with water, which is applied and sponged off several times to allow it to penetrate into the plaster, so that when the plaster to form the casing is poured into the original mould the surfaces are easily separated.

117 Setting up a pattern for
industrial 'Block and case' making.

118 First half of mould,
made, second illustrated.

119 The complete casing.

120 Examples of half block,
and full block.

Beaker mould

Your first model should be a simple one-piece drain mould. Try
making a beaker. The pattern may be made from a thrown wheel
shape. When the shape is leather-hard it should be turned and
burnished with a turning tool. It is important to remember that a
finished clay model will shrink considerably in drying and firing and
should be made at least a twelfth oversize to compensate. A plastic
or pottery beaker could be used as a pattern if throwing is too
difficult.

Place the beaker pattern wide part downwards on a glass plate or
wooden board and surround with a piece of card or lino, leaving
a gap of an inch or so between card and pattern.

Seal around the edges with soft clay to prevent the plaster escaping
and ensure that the card or lino joining is secure. Pour in the plaster
and the mould is made. If kept in a warm room the mould will be
ready in two or three days. Do not assist the drying by placing in a
kiln or oven as this will affect the plaster adversely.

121 Beaker pattern on right   *122 Fixing the handle.*
of picture. First cast being
poured.

Handles

If a handle has not been incorporated in the beaker pattern, then it
may be made by several methods. The first and most obvious is by
'pulling', when a piece of soft clay is held in the palm of the hand
and gently pulled, stretched and stroked with the other wet hand. It
may be allowed to harden slightly for safer handling before attaching
to the beaker. Better to fasten a soft handle to a leather-hard pot
than vice versa.

It is possible to make a handle mould, which may then be used
either to press or pour to fashion a handle (see Fig. 122).

Plaster of Paris

Before attempting to make your mould for slip-casting, it would be
interesting to know more about the properties of the material. Plaster
of Paris is produced from gypsum rock. Gypsum is a white rock of
great geological age whose scientific name is calcium sulphate. If a
piece of gypsum rock is ground to a fine powder and heated it will
lose about 75 per cent. of its water content. If this powder is then
remixed with water the paste or slurry will set very hard. The reason
for this is that the chemically combined water, previously removed,
has recombined, and the material has reverted to the original composition of rock. The powder known now as plaster of Paris is so
named because the city of Paris was built over ground which con-
tained gypsum; this has been mined and quarried particularly in the
district of Montmartre.

Calcination

One method of producing plaster of Paris from gypsum rock is by 'boiling'. A 'kettle' or vessel usually 3 m (10 ft) in diameter and 3.6 m (12 ft) high is filled with approx. 10 tonnes (10 tons) of broken rock. The kettle is heated externally with hot gases to a temperature of 320°F. (165°C.). When the boiling is completed the product is discharged into a 'hot pit' and, when cool, ground into a fine white powder.

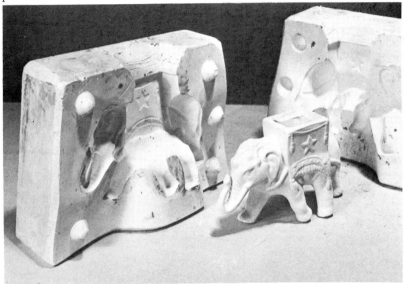

123 Notice how cleverly the mould has been designed. Although only a two-piece mould, the legs have been positioned so that the mould could be made in two pieces.

Mixing the plaster

When mixing plaster of Paris for mould making there are some stringent rules to be observed. Too often students start to stir the water-plaster slurry before all the water has been absorbed. This produces a light-weight mould which is almost useless for the slip-casting technique.

A mixture of 2.2 kg (5 lb) of plaster to 1.7 litres (3 pt) of water, or 100 g of plaster to 80 ml of water will give you the correct proportions for mould making. The powder must be sprinkled into the water until completely absorbed. A simple 'rule of thumb' method preferred by many potters is to ignore the ratio of weight to volume of water, and simply add plaster powder to water until all the water is absorbed. If this is done carefully, avoiding stirring until all the water is absorbed, then this will give you an approximately correct water/powder ratio without weighing. The poured mould will have an initial setting time of eight minutes, and a final setting time of twenty minutes.

General rules when working with plaster

1 **Use only clean vessels and tools, completely free from set plaster, otherwise the set will be too rapid.**

2 **Add plaster slowly to the water so that the bubbles of air can escape.**

3 **Leave the plaster to soak thoroughly, and break up any lumps. Do not stir for too long a period or too vigorously, otherwise the time available for pouring will be too short.**

4 **Finally plaster of Paris must be stored in a dry place as exposure to moisture will cause particles of set plaster to form in the sacks, resulting in quick setting time.**

Piggy bank (*Two-piece cast*)

Pottery novelties are always attractive, and although this field is covered extensively by commercial concerns it is still fun to design and make this type of pottery. The piggy bank is fairly easy to make and it is possible by careful cutting to adapt the pig shape for other purposes, such as cactus holders.

Being a mass-produced method, it provides scope for trying out different types of decoration for it should not be modelled with the intention of making an animal likeness.

A wooden pattern may be used for the casting method, but it is possible and probably more convenient for some students to model a pig in clay. The main precaution whether clay or wood is used is to see that the model is simple and does not offer difficulties in casting. The legs should be small and tapered so that the plaster mould withdraws easily.

When cutting the clay from the pouring neck, use a narrow knife blade so that the shape for the coins is not distorted.

124 Piggy bank. Slip trailing of leather-hard pot

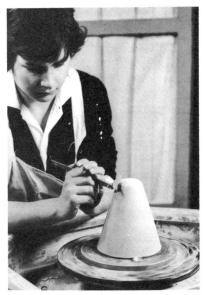

125 Table-lamp base. The sharp edges of the cast being fettled.

A table-lamp base (*Three-piece cast*)

Place the clay cone base down on a bench or board. Set up a piece of lino or stiffish card around it, leaving a space of about 25 mm (1 in) between the cone and card, and fill up with plaster.

When the plaster has set, invert the mould, remove card and treat the flat plaster face with potter's size. Again surround the top of the mould with card and place a small cylinder of clay or wood in position at the centre of the clay cone's base. This cylinder will make the slip-pouring hole in the base. Pour in enough plaster to ensure a mould top thickness of 37 mm ($1\frac{1}{2}$ in). Pour in plaster to a depth of about 37 mm ($1\frac{1}{2}$ in) which when set becomes the top of the two-part mould.

126 Covering the cast with coloured slip.

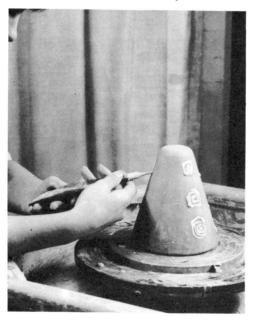

127 Slip trailing.

*128 The finished base.
Biscuit fired.*

A vase (*Four-piece cast*)

If you can get vase shapes turned on a wood-lathe, and made in two halves, you will be able to make this vase mould without much trouble. The alternative is to build by hand and trim a clay model on the wheel.

In the latter case you would need to mark the sides of the vase and build a box around it.

Figs. 129–134 take you step by step through the processes of making a four-piece mould and it will be seen that the two-piece wooden pattern makes possible a perfect edge, so that little or no fettling is necessary on the finished cast.

129 *The first half of the vase in position. Note the special casting box.*

130 *First half cast, and notches cut, dividing size applied.*

131 The frame in position for the second pouring.

132 Both halves cast, frame now set for the base cast.

133 The frame set for top of mould. The gate added to allow for pouring hole.

134 Complete mould with first slip cast model.

Novelty Figures

Loch Ness Monster

It is always fun to model something which is topical, and of course the 'Monster' is often in the news. Again, it must be pointed out that much of the success of these figures and fun-models depends upon the dramatic decoration which oxides and tin glaze can supply.

Figs. 135 and 136 show how simple the model is to make. It is important to follow the glazing instructions carefully for best results.

Method

First roll the clay and cut the base, using brown clay. The 'monsters' are made from coils. The coil should be thicker at the front, which will be the head of the monster, and should taper to form the tail.

The second monster must be smaller and thinner than the first. Bend the coils into humps and lay on their sides to harden just a little. Press two clay shapes to put under the humps for the figures to stand on, paint with brown slip and gently lower the figures into position.

Once the figures are pressed on to the base decoration may begin. This may mean rolling small thin coils of clay for a mane; make a hat if you wish to make it a fun-figure, and press balls of clay along the body and incise.

Glaze decoration

When fired to biscuit at around 1050°C. or slightly above, paint the whole model with tin glaze. The brush must be used with a dabbing action, and glaze applied unevenly. This uneven brushing will allow some of the brown clay to break through when glost fired. Complete the glaze painting before firing, however. Cover the whole with a transparent copper glaze; remember it must be a thin mixture when painting over tin glaze, and finally brush some cobalt transparent glaze along the humps of the monsters. Glost fire at 1060°C.–1070°C.

135 Modelling the monster.

136 The fired and glazed monster.

Fluffy owl

It will probably take the whole afternoon school session for juniors to complete this model. If so much time is not available, or the pot is being made by evening class students, then the unfinished pot should be enclosed in a plastic bag. The bag will keep the clay moist for several days.

Two thumb pots of roughly the same size should be made. Avoid making them wide and shallow since they are to be covered with small pieces of clay representing the owl's feathers. You should work very carefully so that when joined the two pots meet and are efficiently sealed. The aim must be to make a tall hollow shape, narrowing at the top and the bottom. Immediately following sealing, cut a hole in the bottom of the pot; this is to allow air to escape when firing.

Now begins the 'putting on' stage. First model the beak and attach it firmly. Hollow out eyes with your thumbs, and add the owl's tufts to the head. The large eyes might be represented by clay discs cut carefully around a small coin and pressed into the hollows.

The greatest task now, and the most tiresome is the 'feathering' starting from the bottom! Why the bottom? Because like slates on a roof the small feather shapes must overlap, and this would be difficult to do if started from the top. The feather shapes should be made from tiny pieces of clay, rolled slightly pointed at one end and pressed on to the palm of the hand, touched with slip or water, and placed point downwards in rings around the body.

When this has been completed you can use a modelling tool to press the feather pieces; this is first to secure, and second to give a feather appearance or texture.

To finish the model make two feet and press them below the base of the pot. The weight of the body will secure these quite firmly.

137 Modelling the thumb pots.

138 Levelling.

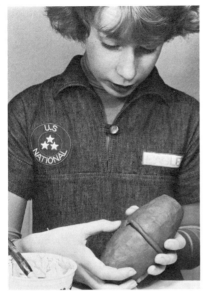

139 Joining.

140 Pressing on the small pieces of clay.

141 Note a finished owl in this picture.

142 Dipping the fired owl in glaze.

Decoration

If either terracotta or buff clay is used the simplest decoration is glaze dipping and painting. The figure is dipped after biscuit firing into a brown glaze, such as iron oxide, Crystalline chestnut or Rockingham brown. Then parts of the front may be painted with yellow glaze, or tin, or both. Eyes of course should have a black pupil with a bright yellow surround.

Indian squaw

This is a very popular little figure which was originally devised by Mrs. Audrey Gregson of the Lune Dale Potteries near Lancaster. It has been made countless times by primary school children, by handicapped adults and by psychiatric hospital patients. It is simply conceived, and as with many other models simplicity leads to success. It is necessary to make a small thumb pot. A ball of clay the size of a tennis-ball will make the base on which to model the head and head-dress. Here, in step by step method, is how the model is constructed.

1 **A thumb pot 60–75 mm (2½–3 in) high made from Staffordshire Red clay.**

2 **A small ball of clay for the head. Pinch the eyes and form the nose with one movement. Press a finger below the nose to represent the mouth. Paint with slip and press the head on to the top of the thumb pot.**

3 **Make a round flat hat, and attach a feather, paint with slip and press on top of head.**

4 **Roll a coil of clay, narrowed at the ends, and slightly larger than a large cigar. Roll very thinly between rulers and wrap around the figure, trying for size (see Fig. 144). When correct size is determined decorate with incise decoration and then wrap the blanket of clay around the figure.**

5 **The blanket must be full enough to allow a small ball of clay, pinched to represent a child's head, to be inserted behind the squaw's head, as though she were carrying a child in papoose manner on her back.**

6 **Take two balls of clay and model her moccasins, place underneath the skirt, positioning them correctly, and smooth into inside of pot.**

7 **Make two plaits from thinly rolled coils and fix them to the side of the head.**

8 **Decoration. When fired to biscuit dip in tin glaze. This is all the decoration the figure needs, as the incised and uneven modelling will show signs of brown through the tin glaze. If colour is desired, the edges of the shawl and hat and feather could be dab-brushed with a mixture of thin transparent glaze stained with copper or cobalt. Firing temperature biscuit 1050°C., glost 1050°C.**

143 Thumb dress made; head, hat, moccasins and blanket in picture.

144 Putting blanket of thin clay around the figure.

Shawled lady

The shawled lady is a derivation of the squaw with one exception. Between the top of the thumb pot and the head a torso and arms are added (see Fig. 145). Here again are the steps to follow:

1 **Make thumb pot in any earthenware clay.**

2 **Make torso and arms.**

3 **Make head and fix all parts together with slip.**

4 **The shawl must be slightly larger than the squaw's blanket and must be cut in a triangle shape.**

5 **Make deep incisions around the edges of the shawl, and decorate with incise markings. An overall textured pattern could be made by rolling the clay on the reverse side of hardboard.**

6 **Wrap the shawl over the head of the figure, and drape suitably in position. An extra touch would be to put a coil of clay on the front of the head to represent hair peeping from beneath the shawl. Also make 'clogs' to put on the thumb pot skirt. Decorate by glaze or underglaze painting.**

145 Thumb pot, torso, and shawl included in picture.

146 Adding the shawl.

147 Finished models.

Modelling for infants

Where there is a kiln in a junior school, and there are now many around the country, it should be possible and indeed, advisable, that the infant classes have a chance to have their clay modelling decorated and fired. The extra thrill of seeing their models shiny and colourful stimulates the children in a way that no other modelling material could.

A good beginning could be made by talking to the children about some of their favourite T.V. cartoon characters. These can be useful, for observation and interest. No attempt is made at this stage to achieve realism, in fact rather the reverse, for cartoon or caricature figures are usually more interesting.

Start with the basic shape and then think of all the animal, fish and bird shapes it might change to.

1 Penguin   Buff or white clay. White, black and yellow glaze-painted when biscuit fired.
2 Squirrel   Brown clay. Dipped in Crystalline chestnut glaze, and dabbled with tin glaze on tummy and tail.
3 Hedgehog   Brown or buff clay, dipped in grey-brown glaze. Flecked with tin glaze.
4 Seal   Brown clay. Dip biscuited figure in tin glaze or brush this on. Dab with weak transparent glaze stained with copper oxide. Dab cobalt glaze on the back of the figure; this should give a 'wet' appearance to the seal.

You might try a duck and many other animals and birds. The decoration should be simple and choice of clay suited to the figure chosen.

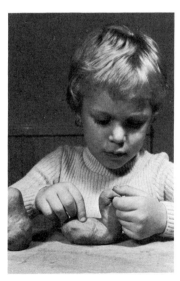

148 *Play school modelling.*

149 *Modelling in infant class.*

150 *A junior model.*

Masks and heads

Whenever clay is given to students to model, and without instruction or demonstration from the teacher, someone at some time will make a mask or a head. This could prove an interesting lesson for all students, and although the suggestions in this chapter relate the positioning of features on mask and head, there is no hard and fast rule which says that modelling should be lifelike. Remembering the masks made by African artists, or the totem poles of the Red Indians, the students should obviously be free to make the masks as grotesque as they wish.

Since the modelling of the mask is achieved by 'putting on', or building up the features by adding pieces of clay, there is a risk of trapping air in the clay, and this could be disastrous when fired. So all additions to the contour must be pressed to the shape sufficiently hard to extrude any air. Start with an oval shape, raised in the middle and tapering round the edges. Consult the photographs as you add:

The nose
Eyebrows
Lips
Chin
Cheeks
Forehead
Hair
Ears

If you can raise an eyebrow, curl a lip or make any alteration to the features, this might give the mask character. Look for difference of bone structure in different races of people—high cheek bones—almond eyes—flattened noses etc. and use these to make the mask interesting.

If the mask is made from a white clay the decoration can be done with coloured glazes or underglaze paints.

A really well-modelled mask might well be preserved by making it into a plaster mould. It would be known as a sprig mould since clay would be pressed into the mould and the mask lifted out with suction by pressing a flat knife on the clay and lifting. Or, alternatively, the mask could be made by rolling a thin slab and pressing it into the mould, or even by using the slip-cast method.

Making a one-piece mould is simple. Just surround the shape with cardboard or lino, leaving a gap of an inch; seal around the edges where the clay meets the bench, and simply cover with plaster of Paris. Some slight modification may have to be made to the mask for moulding to avoid undercuts, since this would make it difficult to extract the mask from the mould.

151 How the pieces are modelled. Partly finished mask.

Armature head

Head modelling using an armature requires some skill. First it will be necessary to make or purchase the armature equipment; Fig. 152 shows how simply the armature can be constructed. If you decide to make it you must make sure that the vertical piece is fastened securely to a strong base. Imagine the weight of clay which sits at the top of the armature, and how this would rock the whole frame if the fastening was not secure. So fix a strong upright on a thick wooden base with large screws. The armature illustrated has a nut and bolt fastening, and the vertical piece of wood is locked into a metal bracket at the base. Holes are drilled across two corners to accommodate the square aluminium wire. You can thread fencing wire through the holes and make a cage. Now cover the cage with polythene sheet and the armature is ready. Decide how big the head is going to be, and make the cage or frame accordingly.

The polythene sheeting serves two purposes, first to hold the clay and prevent it filling the cage, and second to enable the head to be cut cleanly from the cage if you decide to make a plaster mould from your model.

Your first aim is to cover the cage with sheets of clay roughly 12 mm ($\frac{1}{2}$ in) thick. Try to smooth the whole into an egg shape. If the egg shape is tilted, then the narrow portion of the egg represents the chin, and the top represents the top and back of the head. Before modelling, draw two lines across the front of the egg shape dividing the face into three equal parts.

Put the nose in the middle, the eyebrows on the top line and the lips on or below the bottom line. These are very elementary instructions to get you started. When you achieve success through lots of practice you could convert your model into a slip-cast mould by following the instructions in the slip casting chapter.

152 *Preparing an armature.*

153 *Cutting off a head for making into a mould.*

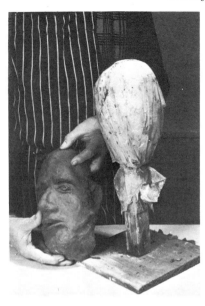

154 *This is how the armature is prepared before modelling.*
155 *(Below): Half of a mould with the completed head.*

Decoration

There is a saying often used by potters in the past—'It's the shape that matters.' This invariably referred to shapes of wheel thrown pottery. But whether you are making wheel, coil or slab pottery it will soon be apparent that decoration is important also. The most aesthetically pleasing shapes will still look ordinary if the decoration is inadequate or badly executed.

There must be great concern by hobby potters and teachers when the problems of decoration are first encountered. You may be wondering whether to plan your designs in advance, or take a chance on making the pot first, and decide upon decoration later. You may do both, and have fun in planning the whole concept of making and decorating, or you may make your pot, fire it and then consider the various possibilities of plain and coloured glazes.

Where students are concerned, particularly examination students, you must of course have a disciplined approach to the craft, and should plan a lesson to give a general picture of the work being attempted.

However, unless students are training for industry they should not be subjected to too much planning, for without doubt this can take away the spontaneity which is so desirable in the art or pottery room. So, a little planning, some free modelling and a lot of determination would seem to be the answer.

Here is a list of some of the many decorative processes you can use:

Glaze decoration	Transfers	Incise and textures
Underglaze painting	Slip decoration	Sprigging
On-glaze decoration	Mosaics	Agate pottery

Glaze decoration

Prepared coloured glazes can be bought from the merchant ready for use, needing only water to be added, or transparent and opaque glazes may be coloured with oxides and glaze stains. Strong colours can be obtained from transparent glazes when 5 to 10 per cent. of stain or oxide is added. In the case of cobalt $2\frac{1}{2}$ per cent. of oxide is sufficient to produce a royal blue.

The opaque glazes of course require more stain for strong colour since the glaze base is modified or opacified with a white powder. They lend themselves to pastel shade decoration and might be used for delicate tinting of pottery.

Oxides have unusual properties, being affected by firing and by the addition of other minerals. Iron oxide may give different colours with different glazes. Chrome oxide usually gives a brilliant green colour. If zinc oxide is present the colour will be brown; if there is no zinc, but large quantities of tin oxide, the colour will be pink. The same metallic oxides may also produce different colours when fired under different conditions. Copper oxide will form strong greens in an oxidizing atmosphere, or the amount may be reduced to form a red glaze under reducing conditions. Reducing refers to the burning of gas or other substances in the kiln at maturing temperature when the kiln is starved of oxygen.

List of oxide colours

Cobalt	Various shades of blue; cobalt with chrome—bluish green; with zinc—cornflower blue; with tin and chrome—purple; with alumina—light blue.
Copper	Green, blue-green. Tin and copper make turquoise. When reduced sometimes makes red.
Chrome	Green, red, pink and brown.
Nickel	Brown, violet.
Manganese	Brown, violet, cream and black.
Tin	White.
Praseodymium	Yellow.
Iron	Yellow, red, brown and black.

Many of the oxides are in the form of black powders and so do not show any recognizable colour when mixed. Therefore when mixing and storing the glazes the containers must be clearly marked. In the case of young students it is often good policy to use glaze stains if practising glaze painting so that they are aware of the colour they are using. On the other hand oxides produce very brilliant colours especially when painted over tin glaze, and the surprise the children get when the fired ware comes from the kiln is often very amusing —and thrilling.

Painting

We usually associate glazing with dipping or spraying, but it is possible to paint with coloured glazes as an alternative to underglaze painting. The process almost follows the pattern of majolica decoration. One interesting aspect of glaze painting is its success in decorating terracotta. For years teachers and hobby potters have faced problems when decorating brown clay. If you dip the terracotta biscuit into tin glaze, or use a paint brush to apply it, you may then paint the model with oxide-stained glazes. The white tin glaze gives you a white background for your colours. Unlike majolica where only stains or oxides are used, glaze paints are weak mixtures of transparent glaze stained with oxides. The stained glazes are usually dabbed on the tin-glazed article, and are brought to life brilliantly by the presence of the tin.

A typical example of glaze painting on tin glaze is the covering of a stone wall pot with tin glaze, usually applied with a brush. Then cobalt and copper glazes are dabbed on the tin glaze in camouflage fashion. Some of the brown clay breaks through the glaze, and combinations of this with blue, green and turquoise produce a handsome finish.

Underglaze painting

This is an old, well tried and successful type of pottery decoration. Its early beginnings were prompted by the development of a white firing body known as Cream Ware, or Queens Ware, and also the refining of materials to provide an efficient transparent glaze. The body was fired to biscuit, a design painted on the pot using oxide stains, and when dry the pot was dipped into the transparent glaze and glost fired. Examination of many early pots decorated this way shows occasional smudging and running of colour, especially cobalt which was used extensively in underglaze painting. This was because the oxide in liquid form dried quickly to powder, and unless an adhesive had been introduced into the colour, powder ran down the pot in the glaze dipping process. Monochrome ceramic transfers were printed on copper rollers, and transfer printing became extremely popular, especially as other colours were added to the transfer palette.

Underglaze painting is not as popular in industry today, probably because it is time consuming and subject to expensive error since, unlike on-glaze colour, it is impossible to erase from the biscuit pot.

The danger of colours smudging has now been eliminated since industry introduced a firing-on process. The colour is now mixed with an oil medium and the ware is fired to a temperature of 700°C.– 800°C. In this hardening on firing the oil burns away and the colour is fixed on the pot. Then when cool it is dipped or sprayed quite safely.

Hobby and school potters usually use gum arabic as a fixative and it is mixed with the underglaze colour and ground on a glass plate or tile. It is usual, and sensible, to dip the biscuit ware in water before painting; this presents a better surface and powder will not build up in lumps to break through the glaze. When painting on once-fired ware the model should be painted at the leather-hard stage. It is sufficiently damp to need no water in the body, and the colour will intensify as the clay dries. A liberal amount of gum arabic should be used to fix the colour to the pot.

On-glaze decoration

The development of the school or hobby electric kiln in the 1940s led to the very popular 'pottery painting' in evening institute and private classes. However, although the processes are simple, and almost foolproof, there is one hazard that is common to amateur and professional alike. That is the fear of 'sugaring' or 'spit out'. This usually occurs only with earthenware, and its cause is still in doubt. The most logical reason seems to be that earthenware pottery which is stored for a long time tends to absorb moisture, and this moisture breaks through the glaze in the form of bubbles at the relatively low temperature of 700°C. When cooling the bubbles burst so that the pot is covered with a sugary texture, and the decoration is spoilt completely. This theory is borne out in industry where no time is lost between glost firing and the decoration and firing of their ware.

It does not seem to happen to china and it would be safe to assume that this is because the body is extremely dense and does not readily absorb moisture.

On-glaze colours are applied on top of the glaze. They are prepared by mixing colouring oxides with frits of low softening temperatures. The oxides and the frit are ground and calcined into very fine powder. The powdered colour is mixed with an oil medium known as fat oil, and applied to the glaze surface. The decorated ware is then fired around 700°–750°C. At this temperature the frits soften and envelop the oxide colour pigments.

On-glaze colours are often referred to as enamels, but should not be confused with vitreous enamels which are applied to copper.

The powder should be ground with a palette knife, and mixed to a smooth paste. Do not use too much oil medium, particularly with reds and oranges, otherwise you may find that when the oil has burned away most of the colour has also gone. Mix a smooth paste, dampen the brush with turpentine and pull off sufficient colour to load the brush.

If you are a beginner you should not attempt to get a flat wash of colour, but rather depend upon flowing brush strokes in your design. To obtain the effect of flat wash you would have to use a stippling technique, i.e. a piece of fine sponge, or a piece of silk or soft nylon enclosing a wad of cotton wool. This is known as ground laying.

Later as the colour dries it is possible to 'scrape through' and obtain your design by the sgraffito method. On-glaze painting is a useful area of pottery activity and provides a simple type of decoration on tiles, domestic ware and figures, needing of course to be applied to white ware for best results.

Transfers

On-glaze transfers have now become extremely easy to attach to

156 *Decorating bowl with underglaze colours.*

157 *Painting kingfisher with on-glaze enamels.*

158 *Applying transfer to white plate.*

glazed ware. Not so a few years ago, when the transfers were known as lithographic transfers and were fixed to the ware with a sticky substance known as lithographic size. The modern transfer is printed on paper, covered with a thin film; when wetted the film, now containing the design, slides easily from the paper on to the pot. Smooth it over with a sponge, and it is immediately ready for firing. These are known as slide transfers.

An interesting development which should interest art teachers and hobby potters is the introduction of special kits for transfer making. Anyone familiar with screen printing would very quickly master the method of designing, and making screen printed transfers. The kits include a frame and nylon screen, a squeegee sponge, transfer paper, stencil film, ceramic printing ink available in twelve colours, and of course a liquid overcoat film which becomes the slide transfer. All these items can also be purchased separately.

Slip decoration

Trailing
The decorating of clay by using clay of a contrasting colour is

probably the oldest form of pottery decoration known to us. Slip decoration, whether by trailing, spotting or marbling, can be rewarding and satisfying.

There are several ways in which slip decoration can be practised. The first, traditional way is to trail lines of thick white slip on to a brown clay background. In the past a honey glaze comprising iron oxide and transparent glaze was used, which gave the white slip a warm honey to yellow tint, and darkened the brown clay. This method is now used by some studio potters to decorate large plates and dishes. There are several types of slip trailers available but for thin, clear trailing a glass tube and balloon shaped bag are the most efficient.

The white slip should be mixed quite thickly and if it proves difficult to brush through the 40s sieve add more water and decant this off as it rises to the top.

Marbling

There is a way of thickening slip by adding vinegar. This is ideal for single line trailing and for spotting, but if used for marbling the vinegar-slip mixture has a tendency to split the coloured slips, which in turn prevents you from obtaining a clear cut division between colours.

Marbling coloured clays on a slab base is very exciting work for young students. The pot should be made in a plaster mould, or a foil container, or any metal plate or shape which will support the clay whilst it is soft. Enamel or plastic ware is not suitable, however, as the clay cannot be removed easily.

When the slab has been rolled, pressed into the dish and trimmed, a brown or white slip is poured onto it and then poured out. The slip must be fairly thick so that the coloured slips which will be added will not move around too easily when marbling begins. The dish is tilted and turned until the slips are mixed into pleasant patterns. At this point a piece of very fine wire can be used to 'feather' lines of slip, giving a most professional look.

One word of warning—the mixing or movement of coloured slips is so fascinating that young students are apt to continue marbling until all the distinguishing patterns have disappeared, and they are left with a grey mess instead of a dramatic pattern.

Spotting

One application of slip which is becoming popular is spotting. It is most successful when applied to slabware such as a flat bottomed stoneware pot, clay discs for mosaics and thin slab made jewellery.

The slab base is covered with a medium thick slip, usually white or brown. Then, using several coloured slips in bottle trailers the colours are spotted, one on top of another over the whole surface of the slab. Bottle trailers or 'dispensers' are most suitable for this type of decoration since they dispense a perfect spot and are easy to control. Here is an example of how to use spots step by step—

1 **Cover the base of brown or buff clay with a thick brown slip.**

2 **Apply dark blue spots all over the area, roughly half an inch apart, and tap the board.**

3 **Cover the blue with spots of light coffee or fawn and again tap the board to spread the colours.**

4 **Spot on top of the fawn with light blue slip, and tap the board.**

5 **Finally apply another spot of dark blue, and tap the board a last time; this will move the spots closer together. With this combination of colours the pattern when glazed is called 'Peacock'.**

159 Trailing.

160 Feathering.

161 Spotting.

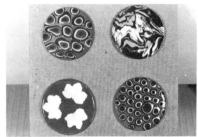

162 Slip decorated finished pots.

Sgraffito

Another traditional slip decoration is called sgraffito or 'scrape through'. A shallow dish or tile is covered with a contrasting coloured slip and allowed to dry to a leather-hard condition. Then, using sharp pointed tools, a pattern is scribed on to the surface; the slip covering is scraped away showing the contrasting colour beneath. The pot is fired and dipped into transparent glaze for glost firing.

Mosaics

There is no way in which a complete description of the craft of mosaic making can be dealt with in this chapter. But if your interest is aroused by a brief description, then you might be inspired to study the mosaic process more fully.

The development of tile and jewellery cutters has made the cutting of mosaic tesserae much more efficient and consequently takes some of the tedium from a time consuming craft. Your first mosaic 'picture' could be made up with a combination of large tiles and small tesserae pieces. This would speed the final result, and of course this is important since the process of mosaic making cannot be hurried. A fine white body should be used as a background for your stained glazes. It might help students to have a step by step guide in as simple terms as possible:

1 **Roll white clay between thin rolling guides and be ready to cut just before the leather-hard stage.**

2 **For large tiles, cut with a 106 mm ($4\frac{1}{4}$ in) tile cutter; the tiles will shrink to 100 mm (4 in).**

3 **For small tiles and background tesserae, use 30 mm ($1\frac{1}{4}$ in) cutter; the clay will shrink to 25 mm (1 in).**

4 **Cut the 25 mm (1 in) tiles twice across the centre producing four 12 mm ($\frac{1}{2}$ in) tiles.**

5 **Fire all your pieces to biscuit, leaving them rather porous to accept glaze more easily. Small tiles do not need to be stacked in the kiln, but may be fired in a biscuit fired dish.**

6 **When design is drawn and colours selected, dip each piece into glaze; place on a kiln batt and fire. If you wish to spray:**

**place on a wooden board and make sure that no glaze
adheres to the bottom of the piece.**

That describes simply the making and glazing process. Now you
need to know how to fix the mosaic pieces to the board. Choose
12 mm ($\frac{1}{2}$ in) thick chipboard; it is superior to other boards and does
not warp. When ready stick the pieces according to shape and colour
by painting with a white glue. Wood workers' glues are excellent.
With modern glues the mosaic pieces may be attached directly to
the board enabling you to see the design as it progresses. A blue
and white design termed English Delft may be produced with tin
glaze and cobalt oxide. The tin makes white and also modifies the
blue to make lighter shades.

Grouting the mosaic

Grouting a mosaic is a matter of choice. Many glass mosaics are
left without grouting between the pieces, but experience with tile
mosaics persuades one that the tesserae look better when surrounded
by a white plaster grout. There is no need to buy special grouting
medium, for plaster of Paris mixed with a little white glue fills the
gaps with a hard white filling. Mix in a saucer one teaspoonful of
white glue to two tablespoonfuls of plaster of Paris plus a little water.
Apply thickly, and scrape over the face of the mosaic with a rubber
squeegee sponge.

163 Cutting small tesseræ.

Incise and textures

One could not imagine a better medium than clay for texturing and in the chapter on slab pottery some texturing techniques have already been described. There are lots of ideas too for incise decoration, and it might be interesting to describe some work which young students might attempt. A square or round tile could be marked on a piece of rolled clay. It should not be cut, but just marked, for it is to be pressed with any small objects that are handy and which might be found in a boy's pocket. Screws, keys, scissor points and handles, pencil ends; all these could be used, and preferably pressed in groups of shapes rather than in a geometrical fashion. Make small areas of incised markings with scissor points etc. until the tile is covered. When you have done this you will notice that the square or round mark will have been pushed out of shape, so the marking which was pressed lightly on the slab originally may now be used as a guide to cut the tile.

When biscuit fired, dip the tiles into coloured glazes. Strong colours such as cobalt or copper are recommended. When glost fired the oxide-stained glazes run into the incise markings, and where the glaze is thicker there is a darker contrasting area of colour.

A rolling pin covered with felt or card shapes, or laced with string alternating with areas of rice, which have all been glued firmly on, will roll continuous textured patterns on the clay surface. These are just two ideas, you will be able to think of many more. These designs are improved by the use of coloured glazes, so try experimenting with pale and dark colours, and with matt and opaque glazes.

Sprigging

The technical excellence of sprigged pottery produced by Wedgwood could discourage the most ardent potter aiming to imitate. There are alternatives, however, which whilst using the same techniques do not result in second rate imitations of Wedgwood.

The sprig moulds used in industry are different from the plaster moulds used by hobby and school potters. They are harder and more durable and, as well as lasting longer than a soft plaster mould, give a finer image to the sprigged shape. If you should wish to try for a finer finish, then your moulds will need to be made from clay and fired. They should not be glazed, but fired rather high for good detail and for sprig extraction.

Still, there is a place for your individual sprig mould. You could model a shape, say a leaf or a flower motif, and make a shallow plaster mould from this. You will see from Fig. 164 that the mould must be shallow, so that the sprig shape will lift easily. Another sprig pattern could be carved from a block of plaster; a suggested design is two oak leaves with an acorn in the centre. This motif could be used to decorate the lid of a trinket box.

Another use for the sprig mould is to make shapes for ceramic jewellery.

It is important too to remember that contrasting coloured clays can shrink at different rates. Natural clays will shrink more than prepared bodies, and although you might have some early success in matching a white clay to a natural clay there is a risk of the sprig motif cracking or even falling from the pot as it dries.

So if a white clay is used to make the pot then a stained white clay should be used to form the sprigged shapes. Or of course buff and brown clays would shrink at the same rate and would therefore be suitable to use with each other.

Some hobby and school potters use clay slip to attach the shape to the pot. This should not be necessary if the two surfaces to be joined are smooth. Water painted on to both the sprig and the pot and gentle even pressure will ensure a safe joining.

164 Lifting the flat shape from the sprig mould.

165 Applying sprig shape to pot.

Agate pottery

Here is a pottery process which seems to be neglected both by industry and by amateur potters. Strangely, it would seem to be the ideal medium for young students to work in, especially if practising and experimenting with colour and looking for the unusual to present to an examiner.

A name which springs to mind is Whealdon, the Staffordshire potter, who experimented with coloured clays and glazes. He mixed coloured clays, modelled animals and then scraped off the surface to reveal the whirling shapes of the mixed clays. Later he resorted to the use of coloured slips to pour over his figures much as we do with marbling.

The craft demands the mixing of contrasting colours of clay. To refer back to the sprigging section, it must be remembered again that the clays used for agate mixing should have the same amount of shrinkage, e.g., brown and buff clays would dry and shrink equally. If you intermix a white body with a brown clay, the surface of the pot will have uneven ridges where one clay meets another when turned, and this could cause fracturing.

If you wish to use other coloured clays such as green, blue or black, then a white clay must be stained either by adding colours to a plastic clay and pugging several times, or by making coloured slips from powder clay. When mixed and sieved the lips are poured into plaster containers and soon become sufficiently plastic to use.

The best examples are made on the wheel. The contrasting clays are rolled into coils, the ratio of one coloured clay being chosen by the potter. The coils are twisted together, wedged, cut and thrown. When the pot is leather-hard it is ready to be turned. As the turnings leave the pot the mixed clays reveal a pattern. This becomes a fascinating game, the danger being that you might go on turning revealing more and more different patterns until the walls become dangerously thin. The Agate pottery is fired to biscuit, bearing in mind the firing temperature of the clay used and then glazed with a high gloss transparent glaze. Some time you might try tinting the glaze with a light shade of copper green or cobalt blue.

166 Collection of Agate Pots.

Ceramic Jewellery

Christmas and birthday presents, school fairs and many other occasions set the potter thinking about what he might make. The potter is better able than most to meet these needs, and making pottery jewellery is another area to explore.

Jewellery shapes can be cut and rolled by several methods. There are special cutters designed to cut and extrude the shapes; small ones will cut cuff-link size pieces, and the large cutters will produce shapes for brooches and pendants. Cutters may be made also from strip tin if a metal-work teacher will co-operate. Sprigged shapes can also be made from plaster moulds to produce various interesting designs.

Obviously decoration is important, and the following short section deals with coloured slips and glaze decoration.

Glaze decoration

White clay is used for jewellery which is to be decorated with glaze colours. Artistic glazes such as Blood Red, Purée Orange and Gold Lustre are used, and applied very thickly on to the white biscuited pieces—ideal for rings, pendants and brooches. Another dramatic glaze treatment means using the little known 'Crackle' glaze. A white shape is dipped into a thin coloured glaze, and then covered with a thick layer of crackle glaze. As the second glaze dries it splits into dozens of crazed shapes. When fired the surface of the piece shows a white shiny crackle, and like a crazy pavement the veins reveal the colour of the first glaze. Aubergine purple and white crackle make a handsome pair for this type of decoration.

The white clay shapes for glaze decoration are cut at the leather-hard stage, and weighted between boards whilst drying. They are then smoothed with sandpaper and the edges rubbed with steel wool. When biscuit fired a favourite and popular decoration is the application of Blood Red or Purée Orange glaze painted in the centre. Surrounding the red is a border of Gold Lustre glaze, again applied quite thickly. The glost firing reveals a bright golden border to a bright red or orange centre.

Coloured slips

Trailing, feathering, spotting

Slip trailing and spotting is described briefly in the earlier part of the section on decoration. Figs. 159 and 161 show this process, and the accompanying tools and trailers. When the thin slabs of clay, rolled between wooden rulers are covered with slip, a design is either trailed or spotted on to the wet slip. The slabs at this stage will be very wet and must be allowed to dry to leather-hard before any further handling. For both trailing and spotting the coloured slips must be in a thick creamy state, so that the liquid does not spurt from the bottle when upturned. Take care too when covering the slab with the slip; as the supporting board is tilted to drain excess slip from the slab, there is a danger of the slab sliding off, so hold the corner of the clay with the thumb until the slip has drained into a container.

The slip-covered slab is now ready to receive the trailed or spotted decoration. If the pot is marbled or trailed you could add to the decoration by pulling a thin piece of wire across the lines to get a feathering effect. The small discs or squares of clay may be cut from the slab once it has dried leather-hard. They can now be handled with safety, and should be placed between boards or small batts so that they do not warp. When powder dry, the backs may be smoothed with sandpaper and the edges rubbed with steel wool. If any of the shapes are intended for pendants, the pendant hole should be cut with a tapered piercer whilst the clay is leather-hard. The piercer is pressed into the clay and turned, making a clean cut hole any size up to 9 mm ($\frac{3}{8}$ in).

Sprigging

Although sprigging is normally associated with wheel or slab pottery, it can be used successfully to make buttons, pendants and other forms of pottery jewellery. Cut flat shapes from thin slabs of clay or model thicker, taller shapes for buttons; place the pattern on a board, surround it with a strip of card leaving a border between card and edge of pattern, and simply cover with plaster of Paris. The mould will dry in a day or so, and can be used to sprig sets of buttons and other forms of jewellery shapes.

167 *Glazed jewellery shapes made from white clay. Note the crackle glaze examples.*

168 *Jewellery shapes cut from slipped clay.*

169 *Sprigged pendants.*

Firing

Firing a new kiln

Makers of electric pottery kilns recommend a first firing of kiln and kiln shelves at approx. 900°C. There should be no pots in the kiln when the strength of the shelves is being tested. Shelves are often referred to as batts, and the supports used to build up the batts are known as props. Another recommendation is that the batts should be painted with a 'batt wash'. This helps to prevent glazed pots from adhering to the batt if excess glaze has been left on the foot. The batt wash will not prevent glaze from flowing due to overfiring, or if you have glazed your pot too thickly, however; thick layers of glaze will run and bead on the bottom of the pot, and could drop on to the batt below.

When you have made your first pots, allow them to dry out thoroughly. If you can rub your finger on the pot and remove clay in powder form then they are 'powder dry' and ready for first firing. Fill the kiln to capacity if you can, and provided the pots are sufficiently strong they may be piled up inside the kiln to fill up all the spaces.

When reading the firing cycle chart supplied by the manufacturer bear in mind that a kiln half empty will reach maturing temperature more quickly than a fully stacked kiln.

Firing

It is sometimes inconvenient to have the biscuit firing during the hours of a school day, unless there is someone whom you can trust to switch off during the early evening. If you forget to switch off the kiln can be seriously damaged. Dry clay pots must have a longer firing than glazed pots which are having their second firing. There is a latent water content present in the clay which must be allowed to escape before the kiln is turned on to the high position, and this can take several hours. In a normal day you would switch on the kiln, turn the switch to low, allow two hours before turning to medium and finally, after another two hours, turn to the high position. The full firing to 1000°C. or over would then take about six hours, making a total time of ten hours.

This amount of time is probably longer than some potters allow, but it is better to be cautious at the beginning.

Overnight firing

One safe method of firing used by some school potters precludes risks of any kind. The switch is placed on the low setting at the end of the school day, or whenever the teacher leaves; it is left in this position overnight, and the following morning the setting is turned up to high. The long firing at the low temperature allows all the water vapour to escape, and the pots are ready for full heat. Some teachers use the medium switch for half an hour or so, but it is not absolutely necessary. As mentioned earlier, a small kiln will reach maturing temperature in six hours, and this means that the full firing is completed within the school day. Leave the ventilator out overnight, and replace it when switching on to full in the morning. Imprisoned water vapour is harmful to the elements and in time corrodes the metal parts of the kiln, so the long overnight heating allows the vapour to escape slowly and is in fact of benefit to the kiln.

Glaze firing

When biscuit ware is covered with glaze and placed in the kiln for its final firing it is known in the trade as 'glost firing'. Since 'glaze is glass', or behaves in the same way as glass when subjected to great heat, it will be obvious that to protect your kiln shelves, and to protect glazed pots from sticking together that certain common-sense precautions must be taken.

1 **Clean off the glaze from the bottom of the pot by wiping. Use thick wet felt.**

2 **Alternatively, use melted wax to cover the foot of the pot before dipping. The wax will resist the liquid glaze and burn away in the firing.**

3 **If you wish the foot to have a coating of glaze to prevent scratching furniture etc. first ensure that the glaze is not too thick, and place the pot on a stilt. Remember though that broken stilts often leave sharp points embedded in the glaze which must be fettled or ground off, and children should not be allowed to handle these pots until this has been done.**

The glazed pots must be stacked separately in the kiln, leaving a space of 9 mm (⅜ in) between. This means that your kiln space will be limited, and you should make full use of your batts and props to build up to the top of the kiln. Another point to remember if only glazed ware is being fired, is that no long period of low firing is necessary, and the whole firing operation need take only six to seven hours. Put the switch to low for half an hour, then to medium for the same time and then place in the high position.

If you have any other type of heat regulator, and of course there are several, then you should follow the same procedure by setting the regulator at the recommended positions for low, medium and high.

Safety

In a memorandum issued by the Department of Education and Science it is emphasized that care should be taken in the handling of all ceramic colours, due to the presence of small amounts of lead, chromium, antimony, etc. which are potentially dangerous.

Whilst most colours are quite harmless the majority contain one or more compounds which can be regarded as toxic. It is recommended that reasonable care be taken in handling all colours, and that strict attention be paid to personal hygiene.

The following precautions are recommended:

1 **Do not introduce ceramic colours into the mouth.**

2 **Do not smoke or consume food while using the colours.**

3 **Do not use colour in dust conditions, or where there are strong draughts.**

4 **Handle the colours carefully, and store in closed containers.**

5 **Use suitable protective clothing.**

6 **Wash hands thoroughly after using the colours.**

Author's note

Copper oxide This ceramic colourant is used by almost every potter to produce a variety of greens used to decorate pottery. It is important that the inside of a drinking vessel should not be decorated with copper oxide. It has been established that certain fruit drinks left in such pots can affect the copper to such an extent when in the presence of lead that it could be poisonous.

Lead glazes There are no longer serious dangers concerned with the use of lead glazes. However, instructions on precautions sent out by education authorities usually point out that in the case of drinking vessels lead glazes should be fired at not less than 1000°C.

Glossary

Agate	Pottery formed from coloured clays.
Alumina	With silica and other materials forms clay.
Ark	Large tank where slips are mixed.
Ball clay	Good quality clay. Added to other clays to strengthen. Highly plastic.
Batts	Fireclay shelves upon which clay ware is placed for firing.
Biscuit	Clay that has been fired once and is unglazed.
Body	Term used to describe a clay to which other non-clay materials have been added.
Borax	Flux for glazes.
Body stain	Prepared oxides for staining slips or plastic clay.
Bulging	Finger pressure on wheel pot to give shape.
Casting	Making hollow ware by the slip cast method.
Calcine	To heat a substance in order to disintegrate, or to reduce it to a powder.
Casting slip	A mixture of powder or plastic clay into which has been introduced a deflocculant—silicate of soda.
China clay	Known as Kaolin, and a primary clay. When mixed with calcined bone and stone fires hard and translucent.
Clay	Decomposed igneous feldspar.
Cobalt	A colouring oxide used for an infinite variety of shades of blue in pottery decoration.
Copper	A colouring oxide. The base for most greens in pottery decoration.
Chrome	A metal oxide producing deep green, and pink when associated with tin.
Cutting off	Passing thin wire beneath pot before sliding or lifting from the wheel.
Crazing	A glaze fault, producing cracks in the surface of the glaze.

Dipping	Complete immersion of pot in glaze.
Earthenware	A low firing secondary clay used for domestic ware.
Enamel	Alternative term for on-glaze colour.
Fat oil	A product left from distilling American turpentine; used to mix with on-glaze paints as a fixative.
Feathering	Trailing a feather or thin wire across slip trailed ware for decorative effect.
Fettling	Trimming cast models where mould joints leave lines of clay.
Fireclay	A refractory clay; will fire to very high temperatures. Often contains grog.
Flux	Lead and borax. Assists in the flow of earthenware glazes.
Frit	Flux used in the preparation of glazes and colours. A mixture of silica and lead or silica and borax.
Glaze	A vitreous (glassy) coating on ceramic articles.
Grog	Ground biscuit clay or sand added to clay.
Glost	A term used to signify when biscuit ware has been glazed and fired.
Ground laying	A flat wash of on-glaze enamel covering a plate or dish.
Grouting	Running a plaster or cement mixture into the spaces between tiles or mosaic pieces.
Gum	Gum arabic, or tragacanth. Mixing mediums for underglaze painting.
Gypsum	A rock from which plaster of Paris is made.
Incising	Decoration. Pressing leather-hard clay with a tool.
Indenting	Decoration. Pressing soft clay with a tool.
Iron	An oxide producing a range of yellow and brown colourants.
Kidney rubber	Mould rubber for smoothing a finished wheelpot.
Kiln	An oven for baking clay to a very high temperature.
Knuckling up	Pressure by knuckle of first finger against the finger of other hand to make a wheel pot 'grow'.
Lead	Flux for earthenware glazes.
Leadless	Term used by glaze makers to indicate that the glaze contains no lead.
Leather-hard	The condition of clay when it may be cut like soap.
Litho	Name given to transfer on which a design is printed for transference to glost ware. Modern method of

	transfer is known as 'Water Slide'.
Majolica	Low firing opaque (tin) glaze.
Marl	Earthenware clay containing high proportion of iron.
Matt	Non-glossy glaze.
Nickel	Nickel oxide used in glazes to produce blues, greens, browns and yellows.
On-glaze	Known in industry as enamels. Painted on glazed ware and fired at approx. 750°C.
Once fired	The term used to describe the method of making painting, glazing and firing in one operation.
Oxides	Strong pure pottery colours from which all stains and pottery paints are produced.
Plaster	See gypsum.
Porcelain	A white, translucent and vitreous pottery.
Pug mill	A machine for reclaiming hard clay.
Porous	Refers to biscuit ware which allows the water in the glaze to penetrate into the body, allowing a thick deposit of glaze on the pot.
Primary	A pure clay, such as china clay.
Pyrometer	A heat recording instrument fitted to kilns to measure the temperature.
Rolling sticks	Used in conjunction with rolling pin to determine the thickness of rolled clay.
Reduction	Starving the kiln of oxygen.
Refractory	A material which can be fired at high temperatures and used in the manufacture of kiln furniture.
Relief	Pattern obtained from slab clay after rolling with a felt roller from which shapes have been cut. Raised decoration.
Rutile	Titanium dioxide. A dark sand; when added to glaze produces a specking effect.
Sgraffito	A method of decoration. The action of scraping through a coloured slip exposing the body beneath.
Sieve	Measured in number of holes to the linear inch. Used in the mixing of slip clays and glazes.
Slab pottery	Method of making pottery by rolling and building.
Slip clay	Clay in liquid state. Often referred to as potter's glue. Used with oxide stains for decoration and also in a deflocculated condition for slip casting.

Slip trailer	A small rubber bag into which a narrow tube is fitted.
Soft firing	Low firing of clay resulting in porous biscuit ware.
Sprig mould	Made from plaster or eathenware for pressing clay shapes.
Sprigging	Fixing flat clay pieces on to a body of contrasting colour.
Stains	Oxides for colouring pottery.
Stilts	Made from fireclay, and used to stand glazed ware on to prevent base of pot from sticking to kiln batt.
Stoneware	A high firing clay. Hard, dense, impervious.
Template	A paper pattern.
Terracotta	Low fired red earthenware clay.
Tessera	Small tile; a piece of mosaic pattern.
Textures	Any mark made on surface of soft clay.
Tile cutters	Metal cutters for making and extruding tiles and jewellery pieces.
Tin oxide	An opacifier used in making tin glaze, and for majolica painting.
Transfers	Screen printed 'water slides'. For fixing to glost ware.
Turning tools	Tools used for turning leather-hard pottery.
Underglaze	Prepared oxides for painting on biscuit ware.
Vitreous	A non porous body.
Weathering	Leaving clay outdoors.
Zircon	A type of sand which when ground and mixed with other glaze constituents produces an opaque, hard glaze.

Acknowledgements

Acknowledgement is due to Jim Handforth; Audrey Gregson of Lune Dale Potteries; Dennis Ward; and particularly to J. Leslie Stokes, who has taken the black and white photographs and colour plate nos. 13 to 19.

Colour photographs are also reproduced by courtesy of the following: Mrs. Ena Cox (1, 2); Kye Grundy (11, 12).

All other photographs have been kindly loaned by Podmore and Sons, Shelton, Stoke on Trent. Plate 7 is reproduced by courtesy of Harry Horlock Stringer, and plate 8 by courtesy of Derek Emms.

All the tools and materials referred to in *Pottery for Beginners* have been supplied by Podmore.

My thanks are due to several members of the Podmore staff, and in particular to Mr. Gordon Slinn for confirmation of technical data.

The following is a list of materials used.

Clay
B.1034 Grogged school
P.1031 Staffordshire Red
B.1024 White earthenware
P.1040 Earthenware/Stoneware

Glaze
P.2104 Transparent
P.2111 Tin
P.2113 White opaque matt
P.2116 Zinc/tin matt white
P.2150 Pewter glaze
P.2146 Golden yellow
P.2151 Rockingham brown
P.2167 Aubergine purple
P.2203 Apollo
P.2208 Crystalline chestnut
P.2213 Crackle base
P.2300 Taggs yard glazes
P.2306 Derek Emms glazes

Oxides
P.3420 Cobalt oxide
P.3405 Copper oxide
P.3410 Iron oxide
P.3415 Manganese oxide
P.3417 Nickel oxide

Underglaze. On-glaze and Glaze and Clay Stains.

Potters' plaster; Rutile; Cornish stone; ball clay; china clay; sodium silicate; zinc oxide; grog; feldspar; borax frit; lead frit.

II